IFISM
THE COMPLETE WORKS OF ÒRÚNMÌLÀ
VOLUMES SIX AND SEVEN

The Odus of Obara
And
The Odus of Okonron

C. Osamaro Ibie

Copyright © 1996 C. Osamaro Ibie
All rights reserved.

Reproduction 2024 by Blacklegacypress.org

ISBN 978-1-63652-434-4

The author and publisher have made every effort in the preparation of this book to ensure the accuracy of the information. However, the information in this book is sold without warranty, either express or implied. Neither the author nor Athelia Henrietta Press, Inc. will be liable for any damages caused or alleged to be caused directly, incidentally, or consequentially by the information in this book.

The opinions expressed in this book are solely those of the author and are not necessarily those of BLP

Table of Contents

IFISM
The Complete Works of Òrúnmìlà
Volume Six
The Odus of Obara

About the Author	**10**
Prologue	**11**
Òrúnmìlà's Revelation On How To Serve the One and Only Universal God	11
Ofun-Iwori Reveals How Òrúnmìlà and Sàngó Helped Each Other	12
The Cooperation Between the Wind Divinity and Òrúnmìlà	14
Thou Shall Not Kill	15
The Beginning of Homicide on Earth	16
The First Strife Among the Divinities	16
The Last Ifá Sage	18
How Chief Obalola Came to Benin	20
Chapter One — Obara-Ogbe — Ebara-Bo-Ogbe	
Obara-Ogbe	22
Ebara-Bo-Ogbe	22
Made Divination for the Corn to Have Children	22
The Divination He Made Before Leaving Heaven	22
He Divined for the People of Illa Orangun	23
He Made Divination for the Hunter	23
The Divination Made for Him Before Travelling for Ifá Practice to the Town of Udo	23
Divined for Òrúnmìlà When His Friend Was Bewitching Him	25
He Made Divination for the Aláàfin of Òyó	25
He Made Divination for the King of Benin	27
He Made Divination for the Children of the Ewi of Ado-Ekiti	28
Chapter Two — Obara-Oyeku — Obara-Bepin	
Obara-Oyeku	30
Obara-Bepin	30
He Made Divination for Sàngó	30
Made Divination for the Son of Oloje to Ascend the Throne of His Father	31
He Made Divination for Statesmanship	32
Divination Made for Him to Liberate Women From a Giant	32
Chapter Three — Obara-Iwori — Obara-Kosi	
Obara-Iwori	34
Obara-Kosi	34
Made Divination for Four Sisters in Heaven	34
He Saved His Son for the Cult of Witchcraft	35

He Made Divination for Fays at Hades	36
What Òrúnmìlà Does to Tie Down Fays or Imeres	36
He Made Divination for Oro (The Secret Cult)	36
He Made Divination for the Oba of Benin	36
This Odu's Special Preparation for Remembrance	37

Chapter Four   Obara-Idi   Obara-Bo-Idi

Obara-Idi	38
Obara-Bo-Idi	38
He Made Divination for the Two Hundred Divinities	38
He Made Divination for the Genitals (Penis and the Vulva)	38
He Made Divination for Ògún	39
He Also Made Divination for Èsù-Obadara	39
He Made Divination for Olókun and Òrìsà	40
He Made Divination for the Small Pepper	40
They Also Made Divination for Awele, the Flirt	41

Chapter Five   Obara-Okonron

Obara-Okonron	42
He Made Divination for the Pounded Yam	42
He Made Divination for the Masquerade (Egungun)	42
The Divination He Made Before Leaving Heaven	43
He Made Divination for the Rubbish Dump (Etitan in Yorùbá and Otiku in Bini)	43
His Problems on Earth	43
He Made Divination for Prince Owolabi of Ijero	43

Chapter Six   Obara-Irosun

Obara-Irosun	46
Made Divination for the Children of Prosperity Before They Left Heaven	46
Òrúnmìlà Declares the Sacrifice for Opening the Gates to Prosperity	46
He Made Divination for the Woman Who Had Six Children	46
He Made Divination for a Mother Having Two Daughters	47
The Divination Made for Him Before He Left Heaven	47
The Dishonesty of His Servants	48
Òrúnmìlà Laments the Unreliability of Human Nature	48

Chapter Seven   Obara-Owanrin   Obara-Lila

Obara-Owanrin	
Obara-Lila	50
The Divination Made for Him Before Leaving Heaven	50
He Becomes A High Chief of His Town	51
Divination for Òrúnmìlà on Caution	51
Made Divination for the Man Who Caught a Treasured Bird	51
He Made Divination for the Hunter	51
He Made Divination for Olobara	52

Chapter Eight — Obara-Ogunda

Obara-Ogunda	53
He Made Divination for Deyi the Livestock Farmer	53
Made Divination for Agbe and Onne	53
He Made Divination for Gberesi Before She Got Married	54
He Made Divination for Sixteen Witches	54
He Made Divination for the Oba and the People of Idanren	55

Chapter Nine — Obara-Osa

Obara-Osa	56
The Sacrifice He Made Before Running Away From Heaven	56
His Encounter With the Cult of Witchcraft	56
Made Divination for the Father of Ojulewa	57
He Made Divination for Òrúnmìlà to Become Victorious at War	57
Divination for Long Life and Prosperity	58

Chapter Ten — Obara-Etura

Obara-Etura	59
He Made Divination for the Head	59
He Also Made Divination for the Trumpet (Ukpe)	59
He Made Divination for Three Brothers	59
Divined for Òrúnmìlà When His Farm Was Being Plundered	60
He Made Divination for the People of Aiyetoro	61

Chapter Eleven — Obara-Irete

Obara-Irete	62
He Made Divination for Plants to Become Trees	62
The Divination He Made Before Leaving Heaven	62
He Made Divination for Onitiide	62
The Contest for Supremacy Between Èsù and the Two Hundred Divinities	63
Divination for Sàngó When He Was Indisposed	64

Chapter Twelve — Obara-Eka

Obara-Eka	65
His Harrowing Childhood	65
He Made Divination for Olofin to Avoid War	66
He Made Divination for the Setting Sun	66
Made Divination for Olofin	66
Sacrifice Against Enmity	66
Divination Before He Left Heaven	67
He Made Divination for Alara-Isa, Omo Ajigbolu	67
He Made Divination for the Owa of Ijesha	67
Divinations for the Olowo of Owo, Ewi of Ado and the Ajero of Ijero	68

Chapter Thirteen — Obara-Eturukpon

Obara-Eturukpon	69
He Made Divinations for the Soldier-Ants, Earthworm and the Fly	69

He Made divination for the Elephant	69
He Made Divination for the Fay or Elf	70
Made Divination for Sàngó	71
He Made Divination for Olobara	71
He Made Divination for the Pumpkin and His Three Brothers	72
He Was Also Having Problems With Marriage	72

Chapter Fourteen   Obara-Ose   Obara-Seke   Obara-Opere

Obara-Ose	74
Obara-Seke	74
Obara-Opere	74
The Divination He Made Before Leaving Heaven	74
He Made Divination for the Two Men Who Learned How to Make Tribal Marks	75
He Made Divination for Okpere, the Slave of Onidoko	75
He Made Divination for Onidoko	76
Divination for Him When He Was Going on Tour	76
He Made Divination for the Mother of Ògún	77

Chapter Fifteen   Obara-Ofun   Obara-Mo-Ofun

Obara-Ofun	
Obara-Mo-Ofun	79
Made Divination for the Parrot When He Tried to Learn Ifá	79
Divination for Him Before Leaving Heaven	79
He Made Divination for Ataparapa, the Armed Bandit	80
Made Divination for Òrìsà-Nlá When Coming to the World	81
He Divined for his Wife to Have a Child	81
Made Divination for Majawote, the Mother of the Sun	81
Made Divination for Igbayinrin When She Divorced Her Husband	81
He Made Divination for the Oba of Benin	82

IFISM
The Complete Works of Òrúnmìlà
Volume Seven
The Odus of Okonron

Chapter One   Okonron-Ogbe   Okonron-Mi-Sode
Okonron-Ohun-Olode

Okonron-Ogbe	85
Okonron-Mi-Sode	85
Okonron-Ohun-Olode	85
He Made Divination for the Two Hundred Divinities When They Tried to Bring Prosperity to the World	85
The Divination He Made Before Leaving Heaven	86

How He Solved the Problem of Having Children	87
Made Divination for Elekole When His Dog Was Missing	87
Made Divination for Eda Lausa When He Was Very Poor	87
Made Divination for Ololo, the King of Fays or Elfs	88
Òrúnmìlà Declares Ude As An All-Purpose Protector	89

Chapter Two Okonron-Oyeku Okonron-Aronmo

Okonron-Oyeku	90
Okonron-Aronmo	90
Divination Before Leaving Heaven	90
He Made Divination for Odogbonikere	90
The Special Features of Okonron-Oyeku	91
Made Divination for the Statesman to Have Authority	91
He Reveals How Òrúnmìlà Left the World for Heaven	92
Ono-Ifá for a Peaceful and Prosperous Life	92
Divined for the People of Igbehin and Itori	93

Chapter Three Okonron-Iwori Okonron-Kosi

Okonron-Iwori	94
Okonron-Kosi	94
The Divination He Made Before Leaving Heaven	94
He Made Divination for the Rain in Heaven	94
He Made Divination for Fire	95
He Made Divination for the Leper of Ijaye	95
Special Divination for Okonron-Iwori	96

Chapter Four Okonron-Idi

Okonron-Idi	97
Divination Before Leaving Heaven	97
How This Odù Solved the Problem of Untimely Death	98
He Made Divination for the Oro Masquerade	98
The Divination Made for Him When He Was Going to Buy a Slave	98
He Made Divination for Ògún and Sàngó	99

Chapter Five Okonron-Obara

Okonron-Obara	100
Made Divination for the Pounded Yam (Iyan)	100
He Made Divination for the Mud (Atebo)	100
Divination Before Leaving Heaven	100
He Made Divination for Oro the Wife of Olofin	101
He Divined for the Man Who Used to go to Heaven for Divination	101
He Made Divination for the People of Otumoba	102
Made Divination for the Calabash and the Melon	102

Chapter Six Okonron-Irosun

Okonron-Irosun	104
The Divination He Made Before Leaving Heaven	104

His Experience on Earth	104
He Made Divination for Òsanyìn, the Medicine Divinity	105
Divination for Wealth and Prosperity	105

Chapter Seven   Okonron-Owanrin

Okonron-Owanrin	106
Divination Made for Him Before Leaving Heaven	106
He Later Founded His Own Town	107
He Made Divination for the Dog	107
Made Divination for Sàngó	108
He Made Divination for Alapini Iyan-Iyan, and Ikola	108

Chapter Eight   Okonron-Ogunda

Okonron-Ogunda	109
He Made Divination for Animal-Kind and Divinities	109
The Divination He Made Before Leaving Heaven	109
He Made Divination for Ògún and the Oraclist	110
He Made Divination for Three Ifá Priests With Challenging Nick-Names	110
The Three Awos, and a Fourth One Also Made Divination for the Ifá Man	111
He Made Divination for Eshi	111
He Made Divination for Ajija (Eziza), the Wind Divinity	111
He Made Divination for the Two Babaras	112

chapter Nine   Okonron-Osa

Okonron-Osa	113
Made Divination for the Guinea-Fowl	113
He Made Divination for Oya, Obalifon, Asa and Awodi	113
Divination for Prosperity	113
He Made Divination for the Snake in Heaven	113
The Divination Made for Him Before Leaving Heaven	114
He Made Divination for Sàngó and His House Help	114
He Made Divination for Agbirari, the Friend of Èsù	114

Chapter Ten   Okonron-Etura

Okonron-Etura	116
He Made Divination for the Mouth	116
He Made Divination for the Hand, Throat, Stomach, Anus, Rubbish Dump, and the Sea	116
He Made Divination for the Harmattan	116
He Made Divination for the Dove	117
The Divination He Made Before Leaving Heaven	117
Divination for Him to Have Children	118
He Made Divination for Children Vying for the Throne of Their Father	118
He Made Divination for the People of Otu	119

Chapter Eleven   Okonron-Irete

Okonron-Irete	120
He Made Divination for the Cockroach	120

He Made Divination for the Boa Snake	120
He Made Divination for Water	121
Divined for Orunmila When Òsanyìn Challenged Him	121
The Divination He Made Before Leaving Heaven	122
He had Difficulty in Having Children	122
He Made Divination for the Man Who Married Olofin's Daughter	123

Chapter Twelve   Okonron-Eka   Okonron-Ala-Ayoka

Okonron-Eka	125
Okonron-Ala-Ayoka	125
He Made Divination for the Ground	125
He Made Divination for the Mushroom	125
He Made Divination for the Sun	125
He Made Divination for the Gourd	126
He Made Divination for the Bird Called Agbe	126
The Divination he Made Before Leaving Heaven	127
His Work As An Ifá Priest in His Second Life	128
He Restored the Eyes of the Blind	128

Chapter Thirteen   Okonron-Eturukpon

Okonron-Eturukpon	
He Made Divination for the Horse	130
He Made Divination for Onidiro in Heaven	130
The Divination He Made Before Leaving Heaven	130
He Made Divination for a Seductive Basket Weaver	132
Divination Made for Him Before Becoming Prosperous	132

Chapter Fourteen   Okonron-Seke   Okonron-Ose   Okonron-Da-Ase

Okonron-Seke	134
Okonron-Ose	134
Okonron-Da-Ase	134
Divined for Poverty, Suffering and Deprivation	134
Made Divination for the Snake When He Was Befriending the Squirrel	134
He Made Similar Divination for Akinla	135
The Divination made for Odogbomukere and Okonron-Da-Ase	135
What He Did to Become an Ifá Priest	136
He Made Divination for the Furniture Seller Destined to Become Rich Within Three Years	136
He Became a Member of the Ogboni Cult	137

Chapter Fifteen   Okonron-Ofun

Okonron-Ofun	138
He Made Divination for Wealth (Ajé)	138
He Made Divination for White Rabbits, Hares and Pigs	138
He Made Divination for Òrìsà-Nlá, Oshereigbo	138
Sacrifice for Prosperity	139

He Made Divination for the Monkey 139

The Divination He Made Before Leaving Heaven 139

He Made Divination for the Corpse 140

He Made Divination for Oro, the Divinity of Secrecy 141

IFISM
The Complete Works of Òrúnmìlà

Volume Six
The Odus of Obara

```
  I
I   I
I   I
I   I
```

About the Author

Mr. C. Osamaro Ibie was born in the defunct Benin Empires capital City of Benin in Mid-estern Nigeria on the 29th of September, 1934 to Chief and Mrs. Thompson Ibie Odin. He hailed from a Christian family. When his naming ceremony was, however being performed eight days after his birth, experts in the esoteric analysis of newly born infants, with special reference to the late Chief Obalola Adedayo, who confirmed to journalists when *Ifism: The Complete Works of Òrúnmìlà, Book One,* was being launched in 1987, predicted that God created the infant as a servant to Òrúnmìlà, God's own servant and divinity of wisdom, and that the world was going to know about Òrúnmìlà and the distorted, falsified and fabricated truth about the true nature of the one and only good God through the infant whose future problems and prospects were being analyzed. In fact, Chief Obalola confessed that he himself wondered why Òrúnmìlà left the whole of Yorubaland, which was his base, to come to Benin, which he first visited but could not reside in, to pick his *viva voce*.

According to the author's father the augury was totally ignored as farfetched because the man was talking to a Christian family who could not imagine any connection with Òrúnmìlà.

The author went through his primary and secondary education in Benin City, during which he generally operated as a man-server in the Catholic Church. In 1947, he joined some of his friends to enlist in the priesthood of the Catholic Church, but his father intervened with the Bishop to insist, that his son was not cut out for the Christian priesthood, and the Bishop deferred to the wish of his father by releasing him.

Upon the completion of his primary and secondary education, the author was employed in the Nigerian Federal Public Service where he rose from the post of a Clerical Officer to the lofty position of an Executive Officer in 1959. At the same time, he won a Federal Government Scholarship to read Economics in London. He went to London in 1960 and obtained a Second Class Honors Degree in both Strathclyde, Glasgow and the University of London.

He returned to the Nigerian Federal Public Service where he was appointed as an Assistant Secretary, becoming Deputy Permanent Secretary in 1973 and Permanent Secretary in 1975.

He was appointed as a member of the Nigerian Economic and Finance Committee on the same year, which was charged with the management of the Nigerian Economy. At the same time, he was appointed as a member of the Nigerian Government delegation to the intergovernmental consultative conference between the American and Nigerian governments, on which he served between 1976 and 1980.

Between 1980 when he retired voluntarily from the Nigerian Federal Public Service, and 1989, he operated exgratiation as an economic analyst; writing many newspaper articles on the categorical and hypothetical imperatives of economic policy and management. He also addressed several public and private sector institutions on the directions of economic policy, including; the Nigerian Institute of Bankers, the Manufacturers Association of Nigeria, Nigerian Institute of Strategic Studies, Several Tertiary Educational Institutions etc.

From 1985 till date, he has been serving as a member of the governing Council of the Federal Government owned University of Benin, in Edo State. Since his retirement from the Civil Service in 1980, he has actively engaged in business in the private sector. He was in 1992 awarded an Honorary Fellowship of the Institute of Administrative Management of Nigeria (FIAMN - Hon.) and recognized as a Certified and Distinguished Administrator (CDA).

Prologue

Òrúnmìlà's Revelation On How To Serve the One and Only Universal God:

Òrúnmìlà has often emphasized that the greatest service anyone can render to God is to know him for what he is the exemplar and aggregation for perfect goodness, with no stomach and taste for any evil. Those who associate him with evil are often mislead by the scriptural presentation of a duplicatious and ambivalent Jehovah, who is the embodiment of both good and evil. That deity is a man's conception of an anthropomorphic military commander who must be obeyed under the pain of death. An infallible genius who operates double standards embracing one set of rules for himself and a different set of draconian rules for his creatures. An almighty Father who is quite happy to cast his erring children to a blazing inferno, without admitting that the failure of his creatures to live by his precepts is a betrayal of his so called infallibility and a negation of his omniscience. Incidentally, that is the disposition of the God that it pleased man to create to satisfy his material and political greed and selfishness.

Incidentally, Òrúnmìlà has revealed that the one and only Universal God was neither the creator of Èsù, the Divinity of evil who existed in the primeval of Orima simultaneously with God. Once we are able to move away from the apocryphal scriptural artifice of a God who created a servant who turned round to subvert his good designs, and of the Òrúnmìlà revealed truth that God existed for good as Èsù existed for evil, we will be in a much better position to appreciate what the God of all goodness expects of us.

Since the only Universal God created the divinities and man to live with the evil machinations of Èsù, it really did not matter to him whether his creatures prefer to go the way of evil or the way of goodness.

Òrúnmìlà has revealed that God could not have created Èsù since it is impossible for good to beget evil, just as it is impossible for:- a lamb to give birth to a snake; neither can a hen give birth to a scorpion nor can a cobra give birth to a rat. Good begets goodness as Evil begets evil. Òrúnmìlà has therefore enjoined me to inform the world on the nature of the only universal God of all goodness, who had nothing to do with the simultaneous existence of good and evil. God's one and only son is Truth while the only son of Èsù is Falsehood. Their only point of intersection is in the never ending struggle for the control of the human mind, psyche and soul. It is only God that has the capacity to create, since light, water and air are the only habitats conducive to life. It will be recalled that page five of *IFISM: The Complete works of Òrúnmìlà, Book Two,* gave a pictorial reflection of what existed before God or Olódùmarè began His creative works. The entire darkness of the primeval was the abode of Èsù, which did not conduce to life and growth. In the fullness of time, from his minute translucent enclave, God told light to blossom and illuminate the engulfing darkness. That action of God began the eternal combat between; light and darkness, as well as good and evil.

When asked why God was trespassing on his kingdom of darkness, the creator reassured Èsù that far from trying to annex his territory, He only wanted to create life to thrive in the vastness of space. That was the point at which Èsù vowed to mutilate whatever God created; by turning all human beings to his servants and to feed freely on any vegetation thus created. God did not raise any objection since His preoccupation was the creation of living organisms.

We have also seen at page two of *IFISM: The Complete Works of Òrúnmìlà, Book Two,* how, upon discovering the pervasive and freewheeling influence of Èsù, God created the virtue of intelligence as a compass and rudder for giving directions to us with a wave of the hand, that one has to bribe him off through the instrumentality for sacrifice. No one is happy to give out a bribe to obtain a legitimate right or favor, but when one realizes that it is better to err on the side of conciliation than confrontation, that is when one appreciates the need to give bribes. God himself led the way by making sacrifice to Èsù with snails. Ofunnagbe will reveal later how Òrìsà had to make another sacrifice to Èsù at Orita-Ijaloko when the evil divinity was subverting the good designs of God.

In addition, therefore to the concept and practice of ethical objectivity, God expects us to give to him what is his, which is to be good, and to Èsù what belongs to him, which is sacrifice. This part of the book is mainly concerned with how to serve God. Do we serve God by; praying round the clock for some selfish desires, spending the better part of the day, week, month or year, in a religious house, bellowing praises and flattery on Him in hundreds of names from rooftops, and operating as His death squad on earth in spite of his injunction "Thou shall not kill?" God does not need any of these services from mankind because they make no difference to him. You can only make Him happy by embracing the objective good, living in perfect harmony and concord with your fellow men, and avoiding evil. According to Òrúnmìlà, he likens God to the head of a household, who is happy when there is peace, love and harmony in his house, and uneasy when there are quarrels and conflicts in the house.

The only acceptable service that any man or woman can therefore render to God is to avoid engaging in acts that can make him unhappy. When one resists the temptations to: offend one's neighbor, retaliate when offended; create unnecessary problems for others; engage in whatever one's conscience adjudges to be evil; turn down a request from a neighbor that is within one's ability to oblige; refuse to help a fellow human being who is in difficult; do to others what will make one unhappy when done to one; cheat society or one's neighbor; engage in any act likely to endanger the lives and happiness of others; and to kill any human being for any reason whatsoever, one is truly operating in the true service of God.

It was against the backdrop of these injunctions that Òrúnmìlà taught that anybody who can wake up in the morning to say the following prayer to God consciently and diligently will always be at peace with the Almighty Creator.

As soon as you wake up in the morning and before exchanging greetings with anyone, wash your mouth, hands and face and towel up.

Thereafter go on your knees to pray to God in the Following words:

The Father and Creator of all goodness, I thank you for: bringing me safely to the beginning of another day; putting me safely in a position to report that I did not contemplate or do any evil up to this morning. Do not let me; think of or do any evil from now till tomorrow morning, disobey any of your commandments; and even if I plan or do anything to harm any man or woman, Father, do not allow it to manifest or have any effect. In the same way, if any man or woman plans or does anything to harm me, do not allow it to have any effect on me. I beseech you Father to take my mind over completely and manipulate it such that I will only think of and do the good that you ordained and enjoin us to do, to make me worthy of being called your loyal son or daughter, for ever and ever to the end of my life. Amen!

At this point it is necessary, to examine how the divinities endeavored to operate in the light of God's injunctions and precepts.

Ofun-Iwori Reveals How Òrúnmìlà and Sàngó Helped Each Other:

When Sango's son, Ajayi was critically ill, Sàngó met an itinerant esoteric soothsayer who made divination for him. The name of the soothsayer was, if one does not bend over backward to serve one's neighbor in moments of anguish, one has no right to expect succor from God. The seer advised Sàngó to have his own Ifá in order that the son might become well because the boy was destined to be an Ifá priest on earth.

Although Sàngó was initially reluctant to condescend to approach a fellow divinity for such an obligation, he subsequently swallowed his pride when his son swooned into comatose. As soon as Sàngó narrated his problem to Òrúnmìlà, the latter agreed to prepare Ifá for him. Since Sàngó did not have the requisite materials with him, Òrúnmìlà brought out the ones he had at home. Meanwhile, the ritual was completed and Sango's son became well. That supportive tradition explains why Ifá shrines are today not complete without adornment with thunder stones.

Soon afterwards, Òrúnmìlà had to travel to the town of Ilode for Ifá practice. The king of Ilode had problems in the town which had defied the expertise and competence of all the priests in his kingdom. The king then sent errands to invite Òrúnmìlà from Ife to come to his rescue. Before leaving for Ilode, Òrúnmìlà made divination for the trip and Ifá advised him to travel to the town with a white ram after giving a he-goat to Èsù. He heeded the advice of Ifá and travelled to Ilode with a ram carried by one of his servants.

Meanwhile, at Ilode, the traditional witch doctors who had failed to solve the problems of the town, hatched a plan for embarrassing Òrúnmìlà. On the outskirts of Ilode was an oak tree. As soon as Òrúnmìlà got to the foot of the oak tree, he decided to take shelter and to rest.

Unknown to him there was a meeting of daylight sorcerers being held on the top of the tree. To actualize the embarrassment contrived for him, they broke a branch of the tree and targeted it to impact on the head of Òrúnmìlà, bringing out blood from the injury.

As he was cleaning the blood from the injury, he made a proclamation to the tree that "If the injury it inflicted on his head was accidental, the tree would suffer no retribution, but that if it was a ploy calculated to embarrass him, the tree should wither to its roots within seven days.

The point at which he made the pronouncement coincided with the arrival of the reception party that the Oba had enjoined to receive him overheard his proclamation. He was subsequently led to the town in a grand procession.

As soon as he settled down at the lodging prepared for him, he felt for his instrument of authority from God (ASE) only to discover that he did not have it on him which meant that his proclamation was not likely to be effectual. In other words, the seven days grace he gave the tree would come and go without anything happening to it.

In the meantime, Sàngó had been to Òrúnmìlà's house at Ife to express his gratitude for the effective sacrifice he made to make his sick son well, only to be told that he had traveled to Ilode. Out of impatience not to delay the expression of his gratitude, Sàngó decided to travel to meet Òrúnmìlà at Ilode.

Meanwhile, Òrúnmìlà made a directional divination and Ifá advised him to position his white ram at the entrance to his lodging. He quickly arranged to tie up the ram accordingly. Incidentally, just as the fowl cannot resist the allurement of corn, that is how Sàngó can never resist the sight of a ram. Òrúnmìlà had been assured at divination that the ram was to be used to serve Sàngó who would help to animate his curse on the oak tree. The ram who was being tied to the pillar supporting the main entrance to Òrúnmìlà's lodging when the arrival of Sàngó was announced. Upon seeing the white ram tied outside Òrúnmìlà's lodgings, Sàngó began to wonder what the wisdom of divinity was doing with it.

However, as soon as he met Òrúnmìlà, Sàngó told him that he could not wait for him to return home before expressing his profound gratitude for the good turn he had done to him by saving the life of his son from the shackles of death.

After telling him that he was only too happy to be of some assistance to the powerful Sàngó, Òrúnmìlà told him about his own predicament. He reported that he had conditionally cursed an oak tree that embarrassed him during the journey to town, only to discover later that he did so without the covering authority (ASE) given to him by God. He was therefore hurrying back to Ife to collect his ASE in order to give efficacy to his curse. Sàngó reassured Òrúnmìlà by saying that the situation provided an excellent opportunity for him to express his gratitude in practical terms, provided he would surrender the ram outside to him. Òrúnmìlà lost no time in agreeing to surrender the ram as sacrifice to Sàngó, who instantly took and returned home to Ife with it, after being fully briefed on the appointed day.

On the morning of the seventh day following Òrúnmìlà's proclamation at Ilode, Sàngó dressed up, after having breakfast, in battle outfit and invited his wife Oya to light up the sky for him. Instantly, there was lightning across the sky which enabled Sàngó to target the oak tree at Olode. Back at Ilode, the people had gathered at the main quadrangle of the town to watch how Òrúnmìlà's proclamation was going to manifest.

Meanwhile, the clouds gathered, followed by light drizzles, which was subsequently accompanied by a heavy overcast and sharp lightening, and the bellowing of a thunderstorm. The people of Ilode were flabbergasted to see the oak tree uprooted and carried away to a distance of over five kilometers outside the town.

It was followed by a spontaneous procession to Òrúnmìlà's lodging, to congratulate him. No one knew that what happened to the oak tree was the manifestation of the mutual support and assistance which God enjoined the divinities to give to themselves.

The Cooperation Between the Wind Divinity and Òrúnmìlà:

Òrúnmìlà has revealed why his followers are forbidden to dive into the river and swim in it for a long stretch.

One day after completing the morning rituals, Òrúnmìlà decided to go to river Ogbere to swim. His followers, Uroke, Uranke and Akpako, told him that it was forbidden for a divinity to swim in the river or sea. He insisted that he merely wanted to cool off.

As soon as Òrúnmìlà made his impact on the Ogbere river, Olókun, the Water Divinity decided to punish him (Òrúnmìlà) for daring him without prior clearance. Olókun immediately commanded Ogbere to convey Òrúnmìlà right up to the sea.

Meanwhile, Òrúnmìlà discovered that he was at the mercy of the current which was maneuvering him at tremendous speed towards the sea. By the time he got to Osa river he knew he was close to the sea, which would mean the end of his life.

Almost exhausted, he called on Fefe, the Wind Divinity to come to his rescue. The Water Divinity appealed to Fefe not to mind Òrúnmìlà. Fefe reacted by reminding the Water Divinity that God expected them to help one another in times of difficulty. Thereafter the wind broke the branch of a tree which fell into the river, moving in the direction of Òrúnmìlà. As soon as the tree branch got to Òrúnmìlà, he held on steadfastly to it, and after gathering some strength, he swam out to safety.

The point at which he made the pronouncement coincided with the arrival of the reception party that the Oba had enjoined to receive him overheard his proclamation. He was subsequently led to the town in a grand procession.

As soon as he settled down at the lodging prepared for him, he felt for his instrument of authority. That was the occasion in which Òrúnmìlà forbade his children never to dive into and swim for a long distance inside any river or sea. The first commandment handed by God therefore was for the divinities to be supportive of one another at all times. He told them that He was likened to the head of a household who is at his happiest when there is harmony and concord in the house.

Incidentally, God also told them that they were to do all in their power to prevent Èsù from planting the seeds of discord among them, but that to be able to achieve their objectives, they should learn to keep Èsù at bay by bribing him into submission through sacrifice.

Thou Shall Not Kill:

The second most spectacular commandment given to the divinities by God was not to kill the mortal servants he created at their request to serve them, Death was the only divinity who was authorized to return them to heaven at the expiration of their sojourn.

No sooner did God make that proclamation than Èsù set out to thwart His intentions. Owanrin-So-Gbe has revealed that although it was the expressed intention of God that divinities, man, animals and plants were forbidden to destroy or feed carnivorously on themselves, Èsù did his best to ensure that they did the opposite. According to Òrúnmìlà, this is the strongest authority which exists to demonstrate that anyone who kills his fellow species is doing so in pursuit of the designs of Èsù and not in accordance with God's own injunction.

God explained to the divinities that if He expected men to be killed or to kill themselves, He would not have agreed to create them in the first instance. Therefore, He proclaimed that neither He nor any of His creatures had the privilege to destroy their fellow species. Nonetheless, Èsù had worked out his own strategy for mutilating the designs of God. Èsù went to work on Death to convince him not to mind God because instead of waiting for man to complete his mission on earth before returning him to heaven, he could in fact use him for food because God did not want him to discover that the human meat was the sweetest of all the nutrients He created.

Acting under the influence of Èsù, Death began to attack man only to discover that indeed the taste of the human blood and flesh was *nulli secundus*. That was how man became the staple food for Death. Subsequently, it was Òrúnmìlà who taught man the antidote for warding off the menace of Death, by disclosing what Death forbids. Whenever Death approached to attack men, they would taunt him with his poison, which had the effect of scaring him into instantly to run away.

It was again Èsù who advised Death to approach the four ferocious divinities to be fetching human beings for him. These divinities are Ògún, Sàngó, Shankpana, and Sickness, Death's own wife. First in heaven, and later on earth, Death was effectively checkmated from killing by himself except by proxy through the four ferocious divinities who themselves do not feed on human beings. They only kill for Death and not for themselves, which is why Ògún, Sàngó, Shankpana, and Sickness are derisively referred to as killers that do not feed on their victims.

The Beginning of Homicide on Earth:

It will be recalled that the ninth of the sixteen Olodus of Òrúnmìlà, Ogunda-meji, revealed in *IFISM: The Complete Works of Òrúnmìlà, Book One,* that Ògún was the first divinity appointed by God to found a habitation on earth. For failing to make any sacrifice before leaving, Èsù frustrated his efforts and his mission was a colossal failure. For his mission to the world, God gave him Two Hundred men and women. Unable to provide adequate food for them since Ògún was unprepared for the expedition, his followers became too enfeebled to engage in productive work requiring physical energy.

That provided Èsù an excellent opportunity to work on Ogun's mind for failing to make any sacrifice to him before leaving heaven. Incidentally, Ògún took the physical enervation of his mortal servants to mean a deliberate refusal to obey his lawful instructions and he began to murder all those who could not work. Eventually, he had to return to heaven to report mission impossible.

The water divinity was the next divinity to be assigned to establish a habitation on earth. He had much the same experience of monumental failure. That explains why the metallurgical and water divinities are among the divinities that engage in mass homicide.

Òrúnmìlà was the third divinity who succeeded in founding a habitation on earth because he was able to combine the intelligence of Oba Jagboloro, the Food Divinity with the cooperation of Èsù not only to feed his followers, but also to encourage them to stay happily on earth.

When Ògún eventually discovered that Òrúnmìlà had succeeded where he had failed, he declared an open war on Òrúnmìlà, which he lost woefully, until he sued for armistice. Between Ògún, Olókun and Òrúnmìlà, and with the support of Obajigijigi, Obajomijomi and Oba Jagboloro, the junior Divinities of Plants, Drinking Water and Food, they were able to sustain life on earth.

Meanwhile, all the divinities had come to earth from heaven, but were baffled by the paradox that whereas God had intended to establish an earth insulated from the evil machinations and challenge of Èsù, they nonetheless met Èsù waiting for them on the swamps of the earth, on top of a rock. That explains, why among other things, the shrine of Èsù is traditionally prepared on a stone picked from under the running waterbed of the river. It is called Iyangi in Ifism.

As soon as Èsù dismounted from the riverbed rock on which he had been waiting for God's divinities, he contrived a strategy for inciting God's divinities against one another. Initially, Èsù influenced the divinity of Fear to be gripping prospective victims of Death - which explains why people are usually afraid of Death. That was when Death by himself used to kill his victims with his traditional club (Alugbongbo in Yorùbá and Ukpokpo in Bini).

Following the decision of Death never again to come personally to kill anyone by himself, Èsù began to work on the other divinities. His first victim was the Divinity of Fear which was using convulsion to kill infants. Since fear by itself only kills children, Èsù decided to work on Ògún, the metagalactical divinity who was already producing machetes, spears, bows and arrows for killing animals and birds, and finally convinced Ògún that the same weapons could be used for killing human beings.

The First Strife Among the Divinities

The bone of contention which sowed the seeds of discord among the divinities was the question of who was the most senior. Ògún, being physically stronger and more inventive than others had always assumed the leadership role. Besides, the fact that he was the first divinity sent by God to found a habitation on earth, made him to presume the role of *primus inter pares*. But Sàngó, Sankpana, Water and Night laid equal claims to seniority.

At a subsequent meeting of the five daily divine council, the argument became so stiff that Ògún proclaimed that the matter was going be resolved by war such that whoever emerged as the overall victor would claim the right of seniority.

Next day, Ògún told Sàngó to be prepared to do battle with him. Sàngó lined out his followers armed with peak axes, which can only be useful in hand to hand combat. On the other hand, Ògún armed his followers with boomerangs, bows, arrows, machetes and spears which could be used for distant combat.

Before the commencement of the aggression, Òrúnmìlà reminded Ògún of God's injunction to them not to kill. Since Ògún was already under the influence of Èsù, he retorted by challenging Òrúnmìlà to swallow his sputum lest he (Òrúnmìlà) would become his (Ogun's) first victim.

As soon as Ògún lifted up his machete to use on Òrúnmìlà, the latter used an incantation to the effect that unless Ògún was capable of eating; a snail and it's shells, a tortoise/turtle and it's shell, and a snake and it's scales, Ogun's right hand which held the machete should stay up transfixed without coming down, since the praying mantis never brings down it's hand after raising it to fight. Òrúnmìlà continued, by the same token, the snail climbs the tree and any object but lacks the teeth with which to bite or harm them, while the mini-anthill (Odidimode in Yorùbá and Ulelefe in Bini) wears a cap but lacks the hands with which to position it in place. With that, Ògún was effectively humored. Ogun's right hand was instantly transfixed in the air. He however apologized to Òrúnmìlà by promising never again to attack him or his followers. That confirms why an Ifá adherent can never be a war casualty unless he does not arm himself with this particular protective device (Ayajo).

After being released from his ordeal, Ògún went into battle with Sàngó, whose forces he defeated. That marked the beginning of strife on earth. After defeating all the other contenders through warfare and bloodshed, Ògún imposed himself *argumentum baulinum* as the head of all the divinities on earth. When God discovered how Èsù was using Ògún to subvert His intentions, He dispatched Òrìsà-Nlá to go to the world as his personal representative, surrogate, and spokesman, endowing him with the requisite immunity against the evil contrivances of Èsù, provided Òrìsà-Nlá himself succeeded in abhorring evil.

The Last Ifá Sage

An Ifá guru is one who can even divine without sounding Ikin or throwing Okpelle. If I did not meet him, I would not have believed that God created such human beings. Chief Adedayo Obalola was the expert on Ifá divination inter alios, that my father invited to perform my naming ceremony divination when I was eight days old. In the old days, that is, until the onslaught of the whiteman's meddlesomeness and its twin offsprings of colonization and Christianity, the naming ceremony of a newly born child was an occasion for the parents to have a glimpse into the future of the child, to see it's prospects and problems, in order to take prompt remedial actions early enough. With the advent of Christianity and it's imperialist parent, Africans were goaded into discarding their traditional mores, as fetish superstitions. The result is that the blackman was caught adrift in the uncharted ocean of the whiteman who has neither culture nor tradition, except the vindictive and divisive gentility of a culture based on the euphoric and myopic superiority complex. The black man aped this ecstatic propensity of the whiteman by becoming contemptuous of any article of faith and dogma that did not source from the whiteman, thus rejecting and abandoning his own cultural foundations.

That is why, a naming ceremony in my part of Africa has assumed the chameleonic complexion of a Christian ritual, thus completely abandoning it's more important connotation of an opportunity for preparing the child for a life in which the margin of error and fortuity is reduced to livable dimensions. Òrúnmìlà has already declared that God did not create man to live through life as if blindfolded, which is why he endowed wisdom diviners with the knowledge to guide their fellowmen in their sojourn through life.

I would have dealt in detail with Chief Adedayo Obalola much earlier than now but for the fact that I could not procure his photograph. The photograph at page 33, was obtained from his children as recently as July, 1995. It was this man who told my parents during my naming ceremony divination when I was eight days old that he could not understand why Òrúnmìlà left his traditional stamping ground in Yorubaland to pick this child as the emissary through who the world would know about him. He told me this story in 1972 when I met him on the street and came down from my car to knee down to greet him. When he asked me whether I already understood the Yorùbá language, I told him that try as I did, I could not pick it up even though I had a Yorùbá wife. He stunned me with his response when he said and I quote "Òrúnmìlà is wondering in heaven, how you are going to do his work effectively on earth when you do not understand his language." Since the old man's remarks made no sense to me then, I gave him the equivalent of three pounds sterling at the time and went my way.

Before I left him, he recalled that when he told my father about the same prophesy, during my naming ceremony divination in October, 1934, he too dismissed it with a wave of the hand because my father was a fervent Christian at the time. Incidentally, my father sent for him on critical moments in my life thereafter. The first occasion was in 1944 when I was in primary four and suddenly became crippled on both legs as a result of which I had to stop going to school. The story was previously told in *Ifism: The Complete Works of Òrúnmìlà, Book One.*

It was on that occasion that he advised my father that unless he immediately prepared the first stage of Ifá initiation (putting Ifá seeds in a pot of palm oil) for me I would most probably die before that year ran out. The Ifá was prepared the following day, and I was able to get back on my feet that night, and to return to school the following morning.

The second occasion in which my father sent for him was eleven years later in 1955 when I returned from Warri in a demented condition after missing my way and straying for about eight kilometers into the bush. As soon as the old man saw me, he told my father that my condition was Òrúnmìlà's way of demon strating that after remaining in palm oil for eleven years, his vision had gotten blurred and that his removal from oil was not to be delayed for one more day. My beloved mother went to the market immediately to procure all the final initiation materials. I only realized what was happening and regained my bearings six days later on the day the Ifá priests were interpreting my Ifá to my parents. I was then a fervent Roman Catholic, and these strange events failed to strike the right chord with me.

The third occasion in which my father sent for the man was in 1969, the year I almost took my life after striving unsuccessfully for six years to have another child after having my first daughter in 1960, and becoming totally impotent between June and August, 1969. He it was, who without telling him what had been happening to me, asked me whether, I was a complete man as I stood before him, and whether I had recently tried to take my life. Thereafter, he accused my parents of trying to derail my life by forcing me to marry my first wife contrary to the advice they were given during the final stage of my Ifá initiation in October 1955. That was how he set the stage for the termination of my first marriage in September, 1969, which was an epoch-making event, because that was when the manifestation of my destiny began.

The last time my father sent for him was in June, 1979 after Òrúnmìlà made his first appearance to me at the prestigious Atlantic Hotel in Hamburg, Germany. I neither comprehend the identity of the figure who appeared to me at my hotel room after one a.m. That night, nor what he meant by "Eleri Ukpin" which he called himself. When I narrated my Hamburg experience to my father on getting home, he too did not know the meaning of "Eleri Ukpin". That was why my father sent for Chief Obalola and it was he who disclosed that "Eleri Ukpin" was the name that God gave to Òrúnmìlà after his curiosity seeking disposition made him to spy on God's creative designs. God told him that nothing could be authentic without a witness, which is why Òrúnmìlà's sobriquet of "Eleri Ukpin", means "God's own witness at creation", and which explains why Òrúnmìlà, although one of the youngest of God's Two Hundred divine servants, is the only one who knows the secret of everything and everyone created by God. That was the occasion in which Òrúnmìlà warned me not to allow the middle of 1980 to meet me in the public service because "I do not want to be waving my hands to you behind bars." It will be recalled that after my last Minister escaped into self imposed exile, my successor spent almost a year in detention in lieu of his runaway Minister. Who would have come to my rescue, coming as I do from a minority area of Nigeria.

When Òrúnmìlà subsequently entered my life in the *terra incognita* of my retirement, I went to see the old man in 1982 to tell him about my unsolicited encounter with Òrúnmìlà. His only reply was that there is no armor against fate, nor is there any eraser that can obliterate the designs of destiny. I finally heaved a sigh of relief recently when I met his two eldest children, Oloopa and Ifaalaye, who are now proficient Ifá priests. When I asked them how they came by it since their father bluntly refused to impart his knowledge to anyone during his life time, (I offered to pay one of his children a monthly salary to learn from him but he refused entirely) they told me that he had been teaching one of his children called Ifaalaye in his dream, who in turn taught the rest. I was surprised that they already knew so much about Ifism, which confirms the axiom that selfishness is peculiar to earth, and unknown in heaven.

My final encounter with the old man before his demise was on the 18th of December, 1987, the day before I launched my first book on Ifism. I took four journalists and a cousin, who is a top executive of the Central Bank of Nigeria, to establish a living testimony of what he told my father in October 1934 when I was eight days old, and what he told me in 1969, 1972 and 1979. He confirmed what I have already written above but warned me not to publicize the fact that I was Òrúnmìlà's chosen envoy. He explained that if the eggheads and self-appointed advocates of Ifism knew that there was a real champion and defender appointed by Òrúnmìlà, I could get into difficulties. That is why I have been a little more circumspect in my assertions to this day, because I have no cause to seek cheap publicity.

How Chief Obalola Came to Benin:

The day he told me that he came in bizarre circumstances to Benin in 1915 (he lived to be well over a hundred) I became curious. To satisfy my curiosity, he disclosed that he was invited from his home in Ijeshaland by an Ifá priest called Ajayi, from Ode-Irele, who became a Benin Chief with the title of Azari-Oba of Unu-abehe. He was then an up-and-coming Ifá priest in Ilesha in his early thirties.

He never spoke Bini in spite of his eighty years stay in Benin. It will be recalled that Oba Ovonramwen was exiled from Benin to Calabar after the meddlesome British government destroyed and conquered the Benin Empire in 1987. Following his death in exile, his eldest son, Aiguobasinmwin, in accordance with the Law of Primogeniture, after a brief squabble with a usurper, was crowned as his father's successor in 1914. The death of King Ovonramwen marked the end of the doctrine of "might is right" in the Benin Empire, which from 1341, spanned through the whole of southern and what is now the middle of Nigeria, Dahomey (now Republic of Benin) Southern Ghana, Togo, and Western Congo. The Empire was destroyed by the British interlopers. This is not a suitable podium for rewriting the history of Africa south of the Sahara.

Incidentally, King Ovonramwen's son who took the title of Eweka the second, was misled by his counsellors into believing that the King of Benin still wielded the power of life and death over his subjects in spite of the fact that British colonial officers had all but taken over that role. When one of the Oba's wives called Iyaare transgressed the ancestral convention, the Oba sentenced her to death by summary execution. Little did the Oba know that there were traitors in his domain who were only too eager to betray him to the colonial Resident at Benin. This clique came from the gang of usurpers who had tried unsuccessfully to commander the kinship from the royal family by cozying to the British intruders.

Meanwhile, Lt. Col. John Archer, the British Resident at Benin invited Oba Auguobasinmwin Eweka the second of Benin to appear before him to defend a charge of unlawfully murdering one of his wives. Before he left the Palace to meet the Resident, his diviners (Ewaese) had told him to deny the charge, because everything would be done to belie the allegation.

When the King was asked about the whereabouts of one of the wives in the royal harem, he demanded to know what made the question necessary, because no other human being other than himself had a right to know what went on in his harem. Before explaining the question, the Resident put another question to the Oba, as to whether he was aware that the British colonial authorities and not the Oba, were then the supreme authority over the Benin Empire. The Oba replied with an equally sarcastic remark that he was not aware of the change in command brought about by *force marjeure*, there was no other power on earth that would have removed his father from his throne to join his ancestors in exile. The Oba then went on to add that if the *fiat* of military conquest also gave the Resident the right to probe the royal household of the King, his wife Iyaare was alive and well in the palace. The altercation ended on the Resident's demand to see the woman in two weeks time. The Bini's instinctively explained that the Resident's demand was an abomination because it was forbidden for any commoner, let alone "Ikopotoki" (Albino) to set eyes on the Oba's wives. That was the point at which Lt. Col. Archer (called Asia by the Binis) explained that he had received incontrovertible information that the Oba passed and executed the death sentence on Iyaare without recourse to a fair trial in the newly established courts of law.

The Oba said no more words except to conclude on the note that at the risk of contravening the conventions and usage established by his ancestors, he was prepared to condescend to abide by the Resident's demand in a fortnight, if only as a means of negating the false information given to him.

On that note, the aphorism began in Benin that the white authority was no respecter of anyone.

"Asia nebo o, ohogo no,
Eizenogbe Ohogho no"

On getting back to the palace, Chief Agbeleri, the man who brought up my father, was commissioned to scan the western wing of the Benin Empire, that is Yorubaland up to Eko by the sea, to locate and produce any thaumaturgist capable of producing the live image of a human being. Chief Agbeleri subsequently travelled to (Ode-Irele) in the Eko-Alile (subsequently corrupted to Ikale) who knew a young Ifá priest and alchemist, called Adedayo Obalola in Ijesha-O-bokun.

The two Yorùbá men subsequently came to Benin in the company of Chief Agbeleri, where they were immediately given the assignment of preparing the image of a woman who was to be called and capable of answering to the name of Iyaare. They were given a lodging at the Unaabehe wing of the palace. They completed moulding the image of the woman exactly three days to the day the Oba was required to produce Iyaare. When they used okpa-atori, to strike the image, it spoke, to the astonishment of all present, including the Oba. I am afraid that in deference to the wish of the late old man, I cannot divulge what happened between that day and the morning that Iyaare had to accompany her lord and husband to the Resident's office.

Suffice to disclose that a woman dressed in the outfit of, and to all intents and purposes, bearing the resemblance of Iyaare, appeared at the Resident's office at what was then called "ughebo" and has since become the center of the ring road in Benin, as an antiquity. The woman covered her face with her headtie in consonance with her customary injunction not to allow any man other than her husband, to see her face. When the Resident asked for her name, she confirmed that she was Iyaare, who was an Oloi (queen) in the royal harem of Oba Eweka. Her parents who were in attendance were invited to confirm that she was indeed their daughter. After confirming that she was in fact their daughter, her father was instantly arrested for giving false information to the Resident.

Meanwhile, there was a tumultuous applause in the hall and a procession was spontaneously formed to accompany the Oba and his entourage back to the palace. When the procession however got to the last junction before the palace, that was sequel to that event, named (Urho no kpota na gbunu) (the gate where an unspeakable miracle happened) the woman disappeared never to be seen again.

Thereafter, King Eweka prevailed on the two Ifá priests to remain in Benin City for the rest of their lives. With all that Chief Obalola knew, he refused to impart the knowledge to anyone including his own children. That confirms what Òrúnmìlà once gave as the reason why Afindibo, the white man seems to have a monopoly of the inventive genius - because the white man leaves the secret of his knowledge to posterity while the black man prefers to die with what he knows.

Chapter 1
Obara-Ogbe
Ebara-Bo-Ogbe

```
I    I
I    I I
I    I I
I    I I
```

Made Divination for the Corn to Have Children:

When the corn was leaving heaven, she went for divination to Obara-Bo-Ogbe on what to do to prosper on earth. She was advised to make sacrifice in order to have many children. She was told to serve Èsù with a he-goat and other materials which she was to buy on credit. She did as she was told and after making the sacrifice, she left for the world.

While on earth, she left naked for the farm one morning and the farmer, her husband, planted her in the farm. When she began to produce, she brought forth Two Hundred children at a time, each of them dressed gorgeously. That is why it is said that the corn travelled naked to the farm but returned heavily dressed.

On returning home she rejoiced and thanked Òrúnmìlà for helping her to produce many children and to have many clothes.

When this Odù appears at Ugbodu the person should be told to serve Èsù with a he-goat and kolanuts which are to be bought on credit. He will always have new things and plenty of gifts. After preparing the Èsù of his Ifá, he should serve it with another he-goat. As soon as practicable, he will also serve Ifá with newly harvested crops from the farm.

When it appears at divination, the person should be advised to serve Èsù on account of a gift coming to him. He should be told never to reveal the secrets of his success to anyone.

The Divination He Made Before Leaving Heaven:

He was told to serve Èsù with a he-goat and Ifá with a hen, fish and kolanuts, because he was going to be a chronic debtor on earth, although he was also going to be a practicing Ifá priest.

When he got to the world became a notorious debtor who often made a point of refusing to pay for whatever he bought in the name of Ifá. One day, he went to the market to buy yams. When the yam seller demanded payment, he replied that he would not pay because he bought it in the name of Ifá. He however offered to make divination for the seller any time, in lieu of the cost of the yam. Thereafter, he chanted the following poem:-

Ola ifa m'onje odogbo ni kere.
Eyi nipe ki'nra isu loja ki maa sanwo odogbo ni kere.
Ola Ifá m'onje odogbo ni kere

The following day he went to the market to buy a hen in a similar manner. He bought several other materials subsequently, without paying for them although he often got home to share them with Èsù. He prospered in the process. When this Odù appears at Ugbodu, the person will be advised to buy all the materials for the initiation ceremony on credit. At divination, the person will be advised to buy a hen and yam to serve Ifá on credit so that he or she might prosper.

He Divined for the People of Illa Orangun:

Ebara bo'gbe jije. Ebara bo'ogbe mimu. Ebara bo omo ogbe mole, ki omo ogbe ma ba ku lai lai. Adifa fun won ara Orangun Ila tori Oran ago.

Obara ate and drank to protect the son of Ogbe from death. That was the name of the Awo who made divination for the people of Illa Orangun when they had an epidemic of waist pain. He advised them to serve Èsù with a he-goat. They made the sacrifice and the epidemic abated.

He Made Divination for the Hunter:

Oni jije, Ola mimu, Otunla Orunpun shunpun. Adifa fun ode kekere t'onlo si ugbo ike, t'onlo si eluju ije to fi odo odun showo ain bo.

Eat today, drink tomorrow and perform the remaining chores next tomorrow. That was the name of the Ifá priest who made divination for the young hunter when he was going on a hunting expedition. He was known for being so unfortunate as not to be able to shoot any animal successfully. He was however told to make sacrifice for better fortune, with a cock and a blacksmith's scissors. The Ifá priest fetched the appropriate Ifá leaves which were ground with the blood of the cock and mounted on the scissors. The preparation was marked on his two wrists while he kept the scissors with him.

After the sacrifice he began to hunt successfully.

The Divination Made for Him Before Travelling for Ifá Practice to the Town of Udo:

Eeji de ki mi da keke mi deri. Ojo da kimi terun eshin bo agba. Bi ale ba t'ile yarin yanrin aaka. Adifa fun Òrúnmìlà baba she Awo lo si ode Udo. Aafa arimo oba Udo shaya.

Let me cover my head from the rain with an umbrella. Let the rain stop so that I might pocket my instruments. Let darkness come so that the night insect (Yarin-yarin in Yorùbá and Atiebi in Bini) might sing its night song. These were the names of the three Awos who made divination for Òrúnmìlà when he was travelling to the town of Udo for Ifá practice, where he married the eldest princess of the Oba of Udo, who was a divorcee.

On getting to Udo, he initially lodged in someone else's house. The following morning, he wore his dagger on his left hand and went out to buy eko. At the same time, the princess of Udo was coming to buy eko from the same seller. As Òrúnmìlà bent down to pick up the eko, his dagger accidentally struck the princess on the head, who was also bending down simultaneously. The princess was injured and the injury was bleeding profusely.

Meanwhile, the princess held on to Òrúnmìlà, who was at the same time apologizing for the accident. In spite of his apology the princess insisted that he should follow her home to explain his action to her father. He had no option but to follow her.

When he met her father, he queried him for daring to injure his daughter. He again apologized and explained that it was an accident. When the Oba asked him to identify himself, he disclosed that he was an Ifá priest, bearing the name of Obara-Bo-Ogbe. The Oba however ordered that he should be placed under palace arrest, to treat the injury to the daughter's head and not to leave the palace until the injury healed. He had no choice but to remain in the palace.

He was boiling hot water every morning and evening to treat the princess's injury. Meanwhile, princess fell head over heels in love with him and they began to copulate. The princess who had no child from her previous marriage, soon became pregnant. Although her injury had meanwhile healed, Òrúnmìlà felt morally bound to remain in the palace and see her through the pregnancy.

The women of the harem soon observed that the princess was pregnant, and they reported Òrúnmìlà's seductive behavior to the king. The king eventually invited Òrúnmìlà and his daughter for explanations. The princess confirmed that she had been impregnated by the man he detained to treat her injury.

On his part, Òrúnmìlà, unable to put up any defense, once again begged for leniency. The king was however secretly happy that his daughter was at last expecting a baby. He invited another pretty girl in his household and added her to his daughter to marry Òrúnmìlà.

The over-generosity of the Oba however estranged the Awos of Udo and they began to plot the elimination of Òrúnmìlà for stealing the show from them. First, they prepared medicine to procure skin disease for Òrúnmìlà. Next, they prepared a medicinal knife to poison his footprints to cause him to have elephantiasis. Finally, they prepared a third charm to make him develop leprosy.

Meanwhile, Òrúnmìlà had a frightful dream which made him to embark immediately on divination the same night. Ifá advised him to escape at once from the town before morning. He woke up his wives and alerted them of the developments. He hurriedly packed up, and before anyone woke up he escaped with his wives. While on the run, the conspiring Awos decided to pursue him with their lethal preparations. After walking for a long distance, he decided to perform another directional divination. Ifá told him that his enemies were hot in his pursuit. Èsù told him not to worry because he had not worked for the sacrifice he made previously.

Meanwhile, Èsù waited for the conspirators to enter the heart of the forest. As soon as they had left all dwellings in town and villages behind them and there were no places for shelter, Èsù caused a heavy rain to start falling. Since the conspirators were carrying their venomous preparations in the bags they were carrying on their heads, the rain washed the poisons on their bodies and they were instantly afflicted by the diseases earmarked for Òrúnmìlà.

Incidentally, Òrúnmìlà had at that point crossed the river with his wives and taken shelter. The man carrying the poisoned knife was however determined to advance to the bank of the river to use it on the footprints of Òrúnmìlà. On getting to the river, he discovered that it was completely flooded and there were no footprints to be seen around, and he could not cross to the other side of the river. He was completely dejected and decided to return to Udo.

When the rain subsided, Òrúnmìlà again sounded Ifá, who reassured him that the threat of danger had abated. That was the point at which he rejoiced and began to sing in praise of the Ifá priests who made divination and sacrifice for him in the following poem:-

Eji wewe ni yo'bo ose Awo (twice)
Ojo gidi-gidi ni obo ose ogbe,
Eji wewe ni yo'bo ose Awo.

He eventually returned home safely with his two wives. When this Odù appears at divination the person should be told that he is likely to be arrested for an offence he will unintentionally commit, but that it can become a blessing in disguise if he serves Èsù with a he-goat.

Divined for Òrúnmìlà When His Friend Was Bewitching Him:

Ebara baba, Ebara bobo, Babalawo Òrúnmìlà, adifa fun Òrúnmìlà nijo ti kolo rogodo se ore Òrúnmìlà, to tun ba Òrúnmìlà se ota.

Ebara baba, Ebara bobo was the Awo who made divination for Òrúnmìlà when his companion was wearing the face of a friend, while carrying the heart of an enemy. Anxious to find out the secret of his success, Ekolo professed friendship to Òrúnmìlà which made him to become close enough to Òrúnmìlà to know what he was doing at any point in time. Ekolo was however a witch who used to transfigure into an earthworm to destroy Òrúnmìlà's works and designs. In consequence, Òrúnmìlà's works were no longer turning out right. He was misfiring at every move he made.

At divination, Òrúnmìlà was told to make sacrifice because his friend and enemy had inserted a mark on one of his clothes, having different and shining colors. That mark constituted the light with which the enemy saw the way to Òrúnmìlà's house in the night to damage his works. He was told to make sacrifice with a cock, a pigeon, a snail and a plate of ashes. In addition to the marked cloth or garment.

He did the sacrifice, after which the plate of ashes was deposited outside Òrúnmìlà's house, while the Ifá priest who made the sacrifice went home with the marked cloth. When the witch-friend came the following night, he was confused because the light which he used to see through to Òrúnmìlà's house was no longer in place. Èsù saw the earthworm hovering around Òrúnmìlà's house and asked him what his mission was. He replied that he was Òrúnmìlà's friend, but had lost his directions. Èsù promised to cooperate with him if in truth he came not as a friend, but as an enemy because he (Èsù) was out to destroy Òrúnmìlà. With that reassurance, the earthworm confessed that he came to destroy Òrúnmìlà's latest works. Èsù advised him to scatter the plate of divination powder with which Òrúnmìlà used to perform all his miracles. Thinking that the plate of ashes actually contained divination powder (Iyerosun), because Èsù had meanwhile made it to look as such, the earthworm entered the plate of ashes which immediately cut his body into three pieces. Since the earthworm forbids ashes, he died instantly.

When Òrúnmìlà came out the following morning, he met Ekolo his supposed friend dead in the plate of ashes. It was then that Òrúnmìlà realized that Ekolo had been his enemy all along. He then sang:-

Ewa wo Ekolo. Oti ge kele kele. Ekolo rogodo ti'nba Òrúnmìlà sho'ta.

When this Odù appears at divination, the person should be told that he has a tall friend who is taking keen, but malevolent interest in whatever he does. He should be told that the friend is a witch and an enemy. He should look for one of his multicolored clothes or apparels which has a conspicuous mark on it. He should make sacrifice with that cloth together with a cock, pigeon, snail and a pot of ashes and the enemy-friend will be exposed.

He Made Divination for the Aláàfín of Òyó:

Adifaku, Adifatosi and Adifala-Adifase were the three Awos who made divination for the Aláàfín of Òyó when his ancestral Òsanyìn shrine reacted angrily for being neglected.

Alaafin had neglected to serve his father's Òsanyìn since he ascended the throne. About seven years after taking the throne, an oak tree grew up at the Òsanyìn shrine. In a matter of years it became so huge that it was threatening the foundation of the palace itself. Alaafin subsequently reacted by convening a meeting of the elders at which it was decided to invite the three famous diviners of the kingdom. They were Adifaku, Adifatosi and Adifala-Adifase. They were given the task of suggesting how to fell the tree without doing any damage to the palace.

Adifaku was the first to volunteer to fell the tree within seven days and Alaafin agreed to give him half of the kingdom to administer if he succeeded, but to execute him if he failed. Seven days passed without Adifaku being able to cut down the tree and he was duly executed.

Adifatosi also made the same vow and he too was executed after failing to eliminate the tree within seven days. It was the turn of Adifala-Adifase to try his prowess. Before leaving home for the palace, his wives warned him not to drink in order to avoid the risk of boasting to do what he was incapable of doing.

On the precincts of the palace, he saw a beautiful white ram and wished that the Alaafin could give it to him. On getting to the palace, he drank excessively contrary to the advice of his wives. While in a state of *delirium tremens*, he boasted that if the king would give him the ram he saw outside the palace, he would cut down the tree within seven days under pain of death by execution, if he failed.

The ram was instantly given to him, but he was so drunk that he had to be dragged to his house with the ram. When he woke up the following morning, he saw the ram and when he asked his wives where it came from, they told him what had transpired the previous evening. Knowing that there was no way he could cut down the tree, he decided to fast to death, while locking himself in his room.

Meanwhile, Sàngó his friend noticed that he had not seen Obara-Bo-Ogbe for the last three days, and decided to visit him. When he got to his friend's house, Sàngó was ensnared by the sight of the white ram and secretly wished that his friend would give it to him to make a new furnace because the one he had was recently damaged. When he asked for his friend the wives told Sàngó that he had gone into recluse for the past three days because he wanted to starve to death on account of the empty boast he made to the Alaafin.

When Adifala-Adifase, otherwise know as Obara-Bo-Ogbe, heard the voice of Sàngó he came out looking very pale and miserable. When Sàngó asked why he was looking so anemic, he explained that he was drunk when he boasted that he could cut down the oak tree at the Òsanyìn shrine of Alaafin's palace. Sàngó told him not to worry provided he would surrender the white ram to him. He readily agreed to give the ram to Sàngó, and the latter went home happily with a promise to destroy the tree on the appointed day.

Sàngó killed the ram in his house and used the skin to prepare his new furnace. On the eve of the appointed day, Sàngó lit up his furnace and cast all the equipment he needed for the operation. Thereafter Sàngó told Adifala-Adifase to cause a public announcement to be made that no one was to leave the house the next morning until the tree-felling operation was over. Sàngó also advised him to keep bells and gongs by his Ifá shrine. People did not take his announcement seriously because they were making jest of him that he lacked the hands and the feet with which to perform the task. Even his wives did not take him seriously.

As the sun appeared the following morning, Sàngó woke up from his sleep and went into his inner chamber to dress up. As he was dressing, the sun disappeared from the horizon and the clouds began to gather. As soon as he finished dressing, there was a total darkness and Sango's wife Oya, gave him food and he had his breakfast. As he was wondering whether to use the axe or machete, his wife held out her tray and a gale force wind began to blow. Meanwhile, Oya put on the light (lightning) with which Sàngó was to identify the tree. When he saw the tree, he concluded that it was too small to be cut with the axe or the machete.

He instructed the wife to use her tray to cause a tornado to enable him to uproot the tree. As Sàngó went into action, the wife carried the tree with her tray to a location far removed from the palace. Thereafter, a heavy rain began to fall, and Sàngó returned home to rest and sleep. When Òrúnmìlà saw that the tree was no longer in place, he began to rejoice and to dance to the tune of the music from the palace bells and gongs ringing from his Ifá shrine. He was singing the following song:-

Adifaku Awolise-o Ibaratioye, oloye, ibaratioye.
Adifatosi Awolise-o Ibaratioye, oloye, ibaratioye.
Adifala-Adifase Awolise-o, Ibaratioye, oloye, ibaratioye.
Mogbo, moru, Arima eru lu tu Èsù-oni-igbeni
Ibaratioye, oloye, ibaratioye.
Oni don don ni ma pe'Egungun
Ibaratioye, oloye, ibaratioye.

He was rejoicing because sacrifice enabled him to succeed in felling the oak tree which had defied the efforts of his two colleagues.

When Alaafin was told that Adifala-Adifase was dancing, singing and rejoicing in his house, he wondered what the man was celebrating when he had not even embarked on, let alone accomplish, his task.

When Alaafin looked at the position of the oak tree he was dismayed to see it was no longer in place. The king began to wonder when and how it happened. The king soon convened a meeting of his chiefs and also sent for Òrúnmìlà. In response to the invitation, he replied that he would see the king later because he was still dancing for his Ifá.

Not long afterwards the king sent four men to call him and he came with them. The king thanked him for destroying the tree without any damage. Without any hesitation, Alaafin made him the Shasere and Prime Minister of the kingdom of Oyo. When the king wanted to share his harem with him, he politely refused. When this Ifá appears at Ugbodu, the person should prepare his Sàngó with a ram in order to succeed in a contest which would involve him.

He Made Divination for the King of Benin:

The fame of Obara-Bo-Ogbe soon began to spread to the four corners of the known world. There was drought and famine in Eziagbon (Ibere-aiye, Ile-Ibinu or Benin) and when the king heard about him, he sent for him. His achievement at Oyo had earned him the new nickname of Urule Ameru gugugu.

When he got to Benin he made divination and told the king to produce for two elderly volunteers, (a man and a woman), a he-goat, 16 gourds of water to appease Èsù to end the drought so that prosperity might return to his kingdom. One of the two persons was to be given to the divinity of the Sun while the other was to be given to the Water divinity. The sacrifices were made without any delay.

Almost immediately afterwards things began to improve in Ile-Ibinu. Two rivers appeared in Benin which were named after the two persons who volunteered for the sacrifice. The elderly man was called Ikpoba while the elderly woman was called Ogba. The two rivers exist to this day and they still bear these names. Rains began to fall and harvests turned out well. The Binis became very happy and compensated the Ifá priest, elaborately.

On his way home, he stopped at Usen to make similar sacrifices for them as a result of which river Erede appeared and the quality of life began to improve for the better.

Finally he stopped by at Ukere where the Oba persuaded him to help them. He made divination and sacrifice for them and prosperity returned to the town. River Olo appeared in the town and it became a junior divinity which is served to this day.

He Made Divination for the Children of the Ewi of Ado-Ekiti:

On his way back from Ibere-aiye, Obara-Bo-Ogbe was invited to the town of Ado-Ekiti where the Ewi (king) had just joined his ancestors.

Ebara-bo-gbe jije, Ebara-bo-gbe mimu
Ebara-bo-gbe ki omo ogbe maku,
Ki omo ogbe ma se aisan
Oko wi Orun, aya nwi Orun
Aseji wi Orun po, Eyi da igba owo-owo.

Obara-bo-Ogbe provided for the food and
drinks that saved the child of Ogbe from
death and sickness.

Consequently, the husband and wife were full of praises for Òrúnmìlà.

That was the poem with which Obara-Bo-Ogbe made divination for Lakola, the second son of the Ewi of Ado before he ascended the throne of his father.

He also made divination for the eldest son and heir apparent, Tawose, with the following poem:

Ijo-ki-jo ni ijo asinwin,
Ayo-ka-yo ni ti din-din-rin.

The lunatic dances aimlessly, while
The fool is unnecessarily joyful.

He advised each of the two brothers to make sacrifice with a ram, a piece of white cloth and two bags of money. Lakola, the second son made the sacrifice reluctantly, because he knew that by tradition, the throne belonged to Tawose, his eldest brother. Lakola made the sacrifice because Òrúnmìlà had predicted that he could become the beneficiary of his brother's negligence and complacency. When he remembered those words, he proceeded in earnest to make the sacrifice.

On his part Tawose boasted that the throne was his own by right of tradition. He said that he had already prepared the dresses and paraphernalia of kingship and it was only a matter of days before he ascended the throne. He continued "Who will dare to take the throne from me when my name is the only one known to the kingmakers of Ado. The Babalawo merely wants to take money, cloth and ram from me for nothing. He is a thief, and I will make no superfluous sacrifice."

Meanwhile, when Èsù was told by Ighoroko that Tawose refused to make sacrifice, he decided to contrive a strategy for depriving him of the crown. On the eve of the commencement of the coronation ceremonies, Èsù transfigured into a musical drummer and went with his drum to the home of Tawose. On getting there, he began to sing to the beating of his drum. He sang that it was only Tawose that everybody knew and talked about. "You are the one known to the world and praised by the men and women of Ado. You are supposed to be dancing and rejoicing to alert and reassure everyone that you are fully prepared for your coronation." With that strange invitation, Tawose came out of his house and began to dance and sing to the music.

As soon as Tawose began to dance, Èsù changed to an incantational song:

Maaje ewi ni ola -o
Obara-Bo-Ogbe Tawose
Oun yi oje ewi ni ola,
Obara-Bo-Ogbe-Tawose.

That was how Èsù enchanted Tawose to dance from his house to the palace, round the town and away from the town of Ado. He was so completely enthralled that he danced away from home for three days without eating or drinking. On the third day, he fell down from exhaustion and fatigue and swooned into comatose. That was the point at which Èsù abandoned him in the middle of nowhere.

Meanwhile, all was set for the coronation, but the crown Prince Tawose was no where to be found. After waiting in vain until close to sunset on coronation day, the kingmakers invited the royal diviners to advise on what to do next. Divination revealed that the ancestors had earmarked Lakola for the crown all along. Lakola was accordingly invited for the coronation ceremonies, and he was crowned as the new Ewi of Ado.

It was exactly three days later that Tawose was able to find his bearings. After searching in vain for the mysterious drummer who beguiled him away from reality, he decided to find his way home. He eventually got home to meet the town in a mood of ceremonial ecstasy. When he enquired what was happening he was bewildered to hear that his junior brother Lakola had been crowned as the new Ewi of Ado. It was then he remembered the poem chanted by the Ifá priest, who advised him to make sacrifice.

Rather belatedly, he proceeded to make the sacrifice and he was eventually made the Aremo of Ifaki, which gave him sovereignty over a colony of Ado-Ekiti. His brother did that to make him happy.

When this Odù appears at divination for someone contesting for, or aspiring to, a high position, he should be advised to make sacrifice without any delay in order to attain the position, lest he would lose it to a junior person or subordinate.

Chapter 2
Obara-Oyeku
Obara-Bepin

```
I I    I
I I    I I
I I    I I
I I    I I
```

Omo ewi ni'le ado, Omo Oba ni ode erin
Ajo je lo'ri ewe, Afo sun lo ri ima.
Ajo fi asho oliwe ri'we bo ra.
Adifa fun omo araye, atun bu fun omo ara orun.
Awon mejeji njo she ore po ara orun won losi oja.
Won mu omo won ti ara aye.

The son of the Ewi of Ado, and the son of the Oba of Erin, both ate on a leaf, and on the palm leaves. Both wore light clothes. These were the Awos who made divination for the two inhabitants of heaven and earth when they were going to become friends.

Meanwhile, when the citizens of heaven were going to the market during a period of famine, they left their children under the care of their earthly friends. Before the heavenly citizens returned from the market, their earthly friends killed the children left under their care and ate them. When the heavenly citizens returned from the market, they asked for their children, and their earthly friends replied that they had to kill and eat them when they were hungry. The heavenly citizens did not react violently and their friendship nonetheless continued.

After the earthly citizens had totally forgotten what they did to their heavenly friends, it was their turn to go to the market. They also left their children under the care of their heavenly friends. The latter avenged the wrong previously done to them by killing and eating the children of their earthly friends before they returned from the market. When they returned from the market, they were told that the famine became so unbearable that they had to slaughter and eat their children.

Pandemonium was let loose and a fight ensued between the two sides. The dispute became so rife that it attracted the intervention of the Almighty God. When He asked them to explain themselves, it became clear that it was a case of tit for tat. God however decreed that since an association between the citizens of heaven and earth invariably led to discord, there should be no more interaction between them.

When this Odù appears at divination the person should be told not to trust or befriend anyone in order the danger of losing a child.

He Made Divination for Sàngó:

Alukoso oba oni, oun koobo oba she mo.
Aludondon oba oni oun ko obo oba she mo.
Afon firi oba oni, oun ko obo oba she mo.

Oni ije obara oyeku ye, iwo na gbo obe ri.
Egungun'ale ogbe ron lowo oko,
Obara oyeku ye iwo na gbo obe ri,
Awon ni won dafa fun Sàngó oni ija oole.
Onbe laarin igba te mo omo erun-mole.

The royal sword bearer, the royal trumpeter and the royal drummer, all three rebelled against the Oba and decided to withdraw their services. The Oba asked Obara-Oyeku whether he was aware of any instance in which the family of a concubine demanded any dowry from the lover of the woman.

These were the names of the Awos who made divination for Sàngó when the other 199 divinities decided to ostracize him, and to ban him from attending their meetings. Sàngó went to Òrúnmìlà for divination and he was advised to make sacrifice with a ram, rat, fish, eko and akara. He did the sacrifice.

Thereafter, Èsù got up in the midst of the other divinities and asked them for the offence committed by Sàngó to warrant the harsh punishment meted out to him. No one was able to give an intelligible account of what Sàngó did except to complain that he was too outspoken and forthright. Èsù then reminded them that Sàngó was too indispensable to be marginalised. They agreed to relent and twice invited Sàngó, but he declined the invitation. They eventually trooped to his house for rapprochement. The dispute was subsequently resolved.

At divination, the person should be advised to make sacrifice so that all his friends and relations who have deserted him might return to him.

Made Divination for the Son of Oloje to Ascend the Throne of his Father:

Sokoti Aganbede was the most senior diviner in heaven. He invited the wood carvers of earth to carve a divination staff (Orofa) for him. Ogun's carving turned out to be the best and he won the contest. His triumph however evoked so much enmity that he had to leave his abode to take refuge in a new locality.

Not long afterwards, the Oloje died. Once again, Sokoti sent a message to earth requesting the earthly carvers to carve Ella for him. Since Ògún had already left the place, he was not available to compete in the contest. Ella is a set of sixteen ornamental Ikin (Ifá seeds) having four eyes carved from ivory. In the absence of Ògún, nobody was able to carve the Ella.

Sokoti subsequently proclaimed that anyone who was able to carve it, would be given the throne of the Oloje. The son and servant of Oloje had put themselves forward to compete for the title, as descendants of the Oloje. The Oloje was the only other carver who knew how to carve Ella. The two contestants were told to carve the Ella as testimony to their claims as Oloje's descendants. The son of the Oloje never took any interest in his father's profession during his lifetime. His servant was the only one who understudied him conscientiously.

The son of the Oloje however decided to go to Òrúnmìlà for divination. He was advised to make sacrifice and to go to his father's grave to beseech his assistance. After making the sacrifice, he went with a kolanut and ivory to his father's grave and invoked his father's spirit to help him to carve the Ella if he was truly his father.

On the other hand the servant of the Oloje prepared his Ella but forgot to insert the four eyes. After returning from his father's grave, the son of the Oloje had a dream in which his father taught him how to carve the Ella with the four eyes on it. He was subsequently able to carve the Ella and the two contestants presented their carvings for adjudication.

The judge who was to determine the best carving was Ògún but since he had left the town for long, messengers were dispatched to fetch him. When Ògún eventually turned up, he decided that he was the only contestant who carved like Oloje was the one who inserted four eyes on his carving. That happened to be the son of the Oloje and he was accordingly declared winner of the contest. That cleared the way for the son of the Oloje to ascend to the throne of his father.

When this Odù appears at Ugbodu, the person will be told that he will contest for a benefit with other people. He should serve Ògún with a cock in order to win the contest. He should serve Èsù with a he-goat including the mud-effigies of a man and a woman.

At divination, the person should offer sacrifice to Èsù because of a project he is contemplating. He should also serve Ògún with a cock.

He Made Divination for Statesmanship:

When he was leaving heaven, he was told to serve Èsù with a cock and a he-goat because he was going to become an important personality on earth. He was also to make the sacrifice in order to live long on earth and to avoid premature death through a woman. He made the sacrifices before leaving for earth.

He turned out on earth to become the spokesman of his community. He became so popular that he even began to rank with the king. Meanwhile, he got married to the daughter of the Obstacle divinity (Elenini or Idoboo) who was determined to drag him down from grace to grass.

Incidentally, unknown to him, his wife began to create the impression that her husband was more popular than the Oba. The Oba's attention was soon alerted to the vain glorious proclamations of the woman. The Oba invited him for explanation but before answering the invitation, he made divination and was told to give a cock and a he-goat to Èsù.

When he eventually reported at the palace, he prostrated to greet the Oba and Èsù immediately influenced the chief counsellor of Oba to say to the Oba that the offence for which he was invited was a non-issue because he was not in any way associated with his wife's tittle-tattle. The king readily agreed and at the same time made him the Shasere or Prime Minister of the town.

When this Odù appears at divination or Ugbodu, the person should be advised to serve Èsù with a cock and a he-goat to avoid having a brush with the authorities through the action of a woman. He is a reformer who came to the world to make it a better place.

Divination Made for Him to Liberate Women from a Giant:

Apola igi, Amule gba-gbara-gba were the two Awos who made divination for Òrúnmìlà before he was able to liberate six housewives from the clutches of a giant. The giant had apprehended six women who were washing clothes in the river and had them imprisoned in his cave. All efforts made by the men-folk to liberate their wives proved abortive.

The king of the town invited Awos for divination and the lot fell on Obara-Oyeku to undertake the assignment. He subsequently went for divination and was told to make sacrifice with a he-goat, shaving knife, baton and black soap. He made the sacrifice and was given the club, black soap and shaving knife to hold when going to confront the giant.

The giant had been hiding in the cave since he apprehended the women because he anticipated a reprisal from the town. Meanwhile, Òrúnmìlà went to the cave and succeeded in convincing the giant that no one would dare him but that he was overdue for a shave. He used the shaving knife to give the giant a clean shave. Next, Òrúnmìlà succeeded in persuading him with the help of his gbetu-gbetu (the do as I command charm) to have a bath in the river.

Òrúnmìlà gave him the black soap to use. As he was having his bath, Èsù soaked his eyes with the soap and he became temporarily blind. Òrúnmìlà was thus able to take away the women before he regained his sight. Thereafter, the giant returned to the cave and became a gorilla, which he is to this day.

When this Odù appears at divination, the person will be advised to make sacrifice to prevent anyone from using force or subterfuge to deprive him of his belonging and to avoid being driven out of his town, or village. He should also be advised to be careful in handling matters affecting women and to refrain from seductive behaviors.

Chief Adedayo Obalola, The Ifa Sage.

Chapter 3
Obara-Iwori
Obara-Kosi

```
I I   I
 I   I I
 I   I I
I I  I I
```

Made Divination for Four Sisters in Heaven:

Four sisters decided at the same time in heaven to come to the world. They were: The Tigress, the Leopard, the Zebra and the Bush Cat (Eta in Yorùbá and Edi or Erha in Bini). They went to Obara-Iwori for divination and he told them to make sacrifice with a hen, tortoise and rotten materials. They were also advised to make a feast for their fellow animals in order to command universal respect. More especially, they were to make the sacrifice against the danger of unconsumated fortune (Amubo in Yorùbá and Osobo noma sunu in Bini).

Just before leaving for earth, they were to serve their heads as follows:- Tigress with cow meat; Leopard with bush meat; Zebra with Guinea-fowl; and Bush Cat with rat and fish. The Bush Cat made all the sacrifices and at the insistence of Òrúnmìlà, served her head on top of a hill. The Tigress served her head but failed to do the other sacrifices. The Leopard and the Zebra refused to make any sacrifices.

Soon after getting to earth, all four of them became pregnant, and they all put to birth at about the same time. The diviner who made divination for them in heaven had warned that after they had given birth to children there would be a strong wind blowing through the earth. That was the time when Èsù decided to persuade the wind divinity to destroy all those who refused to make sacrifice.

One morning, the Tigress went into the forest to fetch food for her young ones. She killed an antelope and kept it at the foot of the apple tree. As she moved to slaughter it, a fruit dropped from the tree and startled her. Unwittingly, she stepped over the antelope with her left hand. That meant she could no longer eat the antelope because the Tigress forbids to eat any meat that she steps over with her left hand.

She abandoned the antelope and proceeded to kill a deer. She took the deer to the foot of another tree to butcher, but as she was doing so. A fruit dropped from the tree and she again frightfully crossed the animal with her left hand. Once again she had to abandon it. She could not kill any other animal for the rest of the day and had to return to her house, thoroughly hungry. Just before getting home, the hunter saw her, took aim and shot her, dead. Subsequently, the young ones died for want of milk. In accordance with tradition, the corpse of the tigress was taken to the king of the town.

On her part, the leopard was also shot by the hunter whilst going in search of food to feed the children. When the Zebra saw what happened to her elder sisters, she ran to Òrúnmìlà for another divination. After divination she went about to borrow money to buy the materials for the sacrifice, promising to repay the loans after the first rain of the year. Her lenders were the earthworm, the hen, the fox, her brothers-in-law (the husbands of the Tigress and the Leopard) the hunter and the boa.

After the first rain of the year the Earthworm went to demand the payment of her debt from the Zebra, followed by the Hen, the Fox, the husband of the Leopard and the husband of the Tigress. She told them to wait in her outer chamber while she checked the money she was going to pay them. When the hen saw the earthworm she ate her up. When the fox came to see the hen waiting, he ate her up. The fox was met by the leopard, who also ate him up. It was the turn of the leopard to be met by the tiger who also attacked and killed him for food. The hunter was the next to arrive. As soon as he saw the Tiger, he took aim and shot him, dead. Unknown to him the hunter was closely followed by the Boa who stood behind him when he shot the tiger. After shooting the tiger, the hunter moved backward and inadvertently stepped on the tail of the Boa. By reflex action the boa bit the hunter, who turned round to use his cutlass to kill the Boa. The hunter however later died from the toxic effect of the Boa's bite. Thus, all the seven creditors of the Zebra had eliminated one another, leaving her to pay nobody.

The Cat, the only one who made the sacrifice escaped unscathed. That is why the cat is neither used for any sacrifices nor eaten as meat, and why it raises all its children with little or no problems.

When this Ifá appears at Ugbodu, the person should be asked whether he is one of four brothers and/ or sisters. He should make sacrifice in order to avoid having problems after having children. He should advise his other brothers to have their own Ifá and the sisters to marry husbands having their own Ifá, if they are to live long. At divination the person, if one of four brothers or sisters should be advised to persuade his other relations to make the same sacrifice as himself or herself. Each of them should serve; Èsù with a he-goat, akara and eko; Ifá with hen; Ògún with tortoise; and to make a feast for members of his or her family.

He Saved His Son for the Cult of Witchcraft:

He was himself a witch and the meetings of the cult of witchcraft was often held in his house. He did not disclose to members of his household the type of meeting that was being held in his house. He had a rascally son who used to spy on the meeting. Since the witches knew that the boy was spying on them, they decided to punish him by taking a slice of his intestines and liver after every meeting. The boy meanwhile developed chronic stomach trouble.

When the son was at the point of death he consulted Ifá who revealed that the members of his meeting were killing his son. Ifá advised him to convene another meeting of all the members and appeal to them to spare the life of his son. The meeting was accordingly convened and among those who attended were:-

Etusheshe she to fiinu igboshele;
Arogidigba to finu aodo sarin gbolo;
Agbagba okete to finu ogan shibugbe;
Okperegeji to finu Awo shibugbe.

When he asked them what was the matter with his son, he was told that the boy was often spying on them at every meeting and that was why they wanted to empty his stomach. He proceeded to beg them to tell him the atonement to make for the son's transgressions. They told him to make an effigy of his son with mud taken from an anthill, a goat, eggs and plenty of palm oil. He produced the materials at a subsequent meeting, after which the son became well. Thereafter, they held no more meetings in his house.

When this Ifá appears at Ugbodu, the person is more likely to be a member of the Cult of Iyami Osoronga. He should immediately serve the night with a goat to avoid creating problems for his children non account of the meeting being held in his house. When it appears at divination, the person should be advised to give a rabbit to the night.

He Made Divination for Fays at Hades:

Obara ba le ra Ògún, Babalawo imere, Odifa fun awon onile imere. When he was leaving heaven, he was advised to build his house at the boundary of heaven and earth, a place close to Hades, the land of the Fays (Imere in Yorùbá and Igbakhuan in Bini). He was also advised to serve Èsù with a he-goat at the two hundred road junction, adding two hundred pieces of plantains, yams, pieces of meat, and seeds of corn. He did the sacrifice, after which he built his house near the two hundred road-junction not far from Hades, the land of the Fays.

Whenever Fays were making fly-visits to the earth, they had to drop at his house for divination on what to do to collect maximum benefits during their brief stay on earth. The fays were however not given to making sacrifice which is why Òrúnmìlà knew the secrets of how to tie them down on earth. Òrúnmìlà used to advise their parents on what to do to make it impossible for them to return to their beautiful land of Hades. When they discovered how Òrúnmìlà was obstructing their schedules, they decided to be coming to the world through the parentage of his children and followers, which is why Ifá adherents are prone to having many fays as children.

When the Odù appears at divination, the person should be told that a heavy trick is being played on him but that with sacrifice, he would see the bottom of it.

What Òrúnmìlà Does to Tie Down Fays or Imeres:

Uroke mi lawo ligonrin, oroke mi la wo leturaye were the two Awos who taught Òrúnmìlà how to tie down fays (Imere or Igbakhuan). He was taught the incantation to use to offer a he-goat to Èsù who would hold them down on earth. He was also told to make a feast with a goat, akara, eko and beans. Whenever they attempt to return home to Hades, Èsù would stop them.

He Made Divination for Oro (The Secret Cult):

Obara ni kosi, A Obara wori-wori were the two Awos who made divination for Oro when he was anxious to have a child. Oro was advised to settle in a town far away from his home, where he was to make sacrifice with a machete, rats, fishes, food, palm wine, meat and kolanuts.

He subsequently left to settle in the town of Osi, where he made the sacrifice in the form of a feast. The cutlass was prepared with the appropriate medicines and given to him for safekeeping. He eventually had several children at Osi and at the height of his prosperity, he gave each child a cutlass to dance with him. When Oro bellows at night, he says - Motise ebo obara woi-woi.

At divination the person will be told that his prosperity lies outside his home town if he agrees to make the above mentioned sacrifice.

He Made Divination for the Oba of Benin:

Adaba o ba leri igi, ofo ohun, aro yeke yeke. Adifa fun Oba Ado, oge luwa tonni ohun yio she rikon ara. Oni ki awon ara ile gbogbo wa ma odi yi uleun ka. Awon ara ilu re le ofe da lo ohun. Nigba to re titi, won ko da loun. Oba to Òrúnmìlà wa. Òrúnmìlà ni ki oru ebo weure. Oru ebo na. Nigba to ru ebo ton ni won ba ma odi na.

The Dove stood on top of a tree and began to repeat incantation. That was the name of the Awo who made divination for the Oba of Benin, when he decided to do what no one had done before. He invited his subjects to build a wall round his palace. They agreed to perform the task, but did not proceed to do it. After waiting in vain for them to embark on the task, he sent for Òrúnmìlà for divination. He was told to make sacrifice with a goat.

After making the sacrifice, Èsù went round to announce that the Oba was contemplating to impose mass punishment on the people for failing to carry out his instructions. One by one the subjects trooped out to begin the construction of the wall, and it was completed without any delay

This Odu's Special Preparation for Remembrance:

Lele Awo ile ilele, Lelle Awo ile ilelle, Lele Fue Awo ile Òrúnmìlà.
Adafa fun bara agboni regun nijoti woni Òrúnmìlà koni ni iye rinu mo.
Òrúnmìlà ni baba she bii temi ni, moni bii tire ni.
Òrúnmìlà ni iho merindilogún nii bee ni nu oniyemi ye.
Oni gbogbore lo onlu kara bi aje ire.
Oni boba ti da kemi ogbagbe. Oni ariran aranmi leti.
Oni uye aayemi leere.
Oni keeu ni eja she nso ninu omi.
Bi akiko ba fi aka kan aka, ayere oro ano.
Ebara luko si, maa ko niniye itemi loo. Ebara lu kosi.

Lele made divination for Ilele, Lelle made divination for Ilelle, just as Lele Fue made divination for Òrúnmìlà when people thought that he had lost his memory. Òrúnmìlà replied that they were joking. He proclaimed that rather than lose his memory, he would appeal to the leaves for support. He added that there are sixteen holes in the leaf called Niyemiye, all inside its body, like the small clay pot called Ajere having holes all over its body.

He added "for me to lose my memory, the leaves of Uye and Arinran will remind me because; when the fish enters the water it will lift itself up, and when the cock flaps its wings it will lift itself up, and when the cock flaps its wings it will remember what it did the previous day. Obara Lukosi, do not let me forget." This is the incantation with which Ifá priests remember things.

Chapter 4
Obara-Idi
Obara-Bo-Idi

```
  I        I
I I      I I
I I      I I
  I      I I
```

He Made Divination for the Two Hundred Divinities:

Koin-koin mi ta lu idi. Odifa fun erumole ajugotun, erumole ajugosi ni jo ti won bo le ode aiye. The Odù which reported how the earth was founded. He made divination for the Two Hundred Divinities on the right and on the left when they were coming to lay the foundation of the earth. God had used water to flush out and flood the first habitation of the earth because of the debauchery and moral depravity of its first inhabitants. That was why God destroyed the world with water.

After seven millennia, God decided to make a second experiment for the habitation of the earth. He invited the Two Hundred Divinities and commissioned them to go as a body to make the world a better place. Koin-koin, which was the heavenly name of Obara-Bo-Idi, divined for them, advising each of them to make sacrifices to, Èsù with white cloth, chalk, cowries and red parrot's feather to River Mimikpo of heaven, and Guinea-fowl for their guardian angels.

None of them made the sacrifice, except Òrúnmìlà. The messenger (Arugba) that God sent to the divinities was told to tell all of them to assemble at the divine chamber of God's palace the following morning. The messenger told Òrúnmìlà what to do because he was the only one who remembered to give her food.

When they subsequently assembled the following morning, God gave them the matching orders with instructions not to return to their homes before setting out. Òrúnmìlà was the last to show up and it was he who took the snail's shell that contained the sand that was to solidify the foundation of the earth. By divine permission, he also travelled with Arugba, the messenger sent to the divinities by God. Since there was no solid base on earth, the place having been totally flooded with water, all the Two Hundred Divinities stayed on top of the palm tree that had its roots in heaven and its stem and branches on earth, overlooking the mass of water below.

It was Arugba who eventually advised Òrúnmìlà to turn the mouth of the snail's shell into the water below and the soil that solidified the earth dropped into the water. As soon as they were alighted from the palm tree. Thus began the second habitation of the earth which subsists to this day.

When this Odù appears at Ugbodu, a special sacrifice has to be made with a snail's shell picked from the bush, chameleon, ewe tete, ewe odondon, ewe ero, ewe irorowo, he-goat, Guinea-fowl, white cloth and chalk, so that the person might live to a ripe old age. At divination, he should serve Èsù with he-goat and arrange to have his own Ifá so that he might succeed in a difficult assignment.

He Made Divination for the Genitals (Penis and the Vulva):

Originally, the genitals of animals, like those of plants were positioned on their foreheads, where they were scarcely recognized for any useful purpose. One day, an Ifa priest called Mikiligui was performing his annual Ifá festival at his house near the market. The Vulva (Obo in Yorùbá and Uhe in Bini) was going to the market when she decided to stop at Mikiligui's house for divination. He told Obo that she would prosper if she made sacrifice. He told her to bring a black he-goat, a hen, kolanuts, 3 water yams, 4 white yams, an axe and a cutlass for him to perform the sacrifice for her.

She went to the market and procured the materials without paying for them because, traditionally, no one ever refused to do her a favor. The he-goat, axe, cutlass and water yams were sent to Èsù. After eating the edible items, Èsù asked what Obo wanted and she replied that she wanted to have honor and prosperity. Èsù asked Mikiligui whether he had been fed and he confirmed affirmatively, but added that he would not eat the offerings made to him until Èsù had performed the required favor. Èsù was and remains the only power that can modify or mutilate God's creations.

Before then, anyone who wanted a child made a request to God and He created one for the person or animal. There was a route through which children walked to their parents on earth. Èsù embarked on his task by using the axe to cut a tree to block that route eternally. Next, Èsù invited two persons with the genitals their foreheads and sat them down. He removed the penis and inserted it between the man's legs and removed the vulva from the female forehead and inserted it between her legs, using two pieces of skins removed from the black he-goat to cover them up - which is the human pubic hair.

Thereafter, Èsù brought out his ASE and decreed that from then on, all animate objects created by God should have their genitals between their legs, and that whoever wanted an offspring should no longer go to God but to Obo. He added that all and sundry would from then on have to pay the debt incurred by Obo for the sacrifice she made. That is the debt paid by all those desiring to have children to this day. That is not just the dowry payable, but mainly the cost of taking care of a wife throughout marriage.

When this Odù appears at Ugbodu, the person would be told that he had suffered immensely before his initiation, but that he should serve Èsù with a he-goat, axe and cutlass so that he might prosper from then on.

At divination, the person should be told to have his own Ifá in order to prosper in life. He should also serve Èsù with a he-goat.

He Made Divination for Ògún:

Ebara ji ji ji, odifa fun Ògún oni jan onle ni jo to wa aiye.
Ala iniku kon gira. Ebo oriku ni ko ru o.

He made divination for Ògún when he was coming to the world. He was told to make sacrifice to avoid death on earth. He made sacrifice with 2 cocks, a hen and a dog which is why Ògún never dies.

When it appears at divination, the person should be advised to have his own Ògún in order to live to a ripe old age and so that his name would live forever.

He Also Made Divination for Èsù-Obadara:

Ebara obo odi. Idi omole kayin kayin ile eni ni ta eni.
Ishu omode ta tan onla agbalagba loju kanran knaran.
Adafa fun Èsù obadara nijo t'onlo fi arare kowo lo odo Orisa.

The man who does not stay at home. It is the ant in one's house that bites one. The yam planted by a young man made a good harvest and the elderly one became jealous. These were the Awos who made divination for Èsù-Obadara when he made himself an identured servant in the house of God in atonement for a debt he could not repay. He was told to make sacrifice with 2 hens and 2 pigeons. He did the sacrifice. He had been given the task of catching fish everyday and he was doing it so successfully that after the sacrifice God granted him freedom because he was satisfied with his previous services.

He Made Divination for Olókun and Orisa:

Ebara ji ji ji. Odifa fun Orisa, obufun Olókun.

He also made divination for Orisa and Olókun, when Olókun was boasting that he was richer than God. He boasted that there was nothing God had which he (Olókun) did not have. Meanwhile, the Chameleon told God to authorize him to call off the bluff of Olókun. God accordingly gave the Chameleon the authority (ASE) to challenge Olókun.

Subsequently, the Chameleon went to Olókun to ask him to name the day he was going to compare his wealth with Orisa's. He promised to present himself on the third day. On the appointed day, the Chameleon told Olókun to come to the venue of the contest with all his belongings to contest first with him (Chameleon) and that it was only after he (Olókun) succeeded in demonstrating that he was wealthier than himself (Chameleon) that God would enter into the contest. Both Olókun and Chameleon stood out for the contest while God sat on His divine throne to watch.

The Chameleon was able to replicate the reflection of whatever Olókun wore or displayed on his own skin, until Olókun had nothing more to demonstrate and the Chameleon had not even displayed any of his own belongings. After the Chameleon had beaten him effectively to whatever he displayed, Olókun conceded that God was not only richer than himself, but that he (Olókun) was part of God's own possessions.

At divination the person should be advised to serve Èsù with a he-goat and a mirror in order to win a contest he would be challenged to undertake.

He Made Divination for the Small Pepper:

Obara ko-bo-idi. Idi ko mo'le.
Eje ki koin-koin ile eni ki o ta eni
Adifa fun ata wewe ti o nlo si Ògún-ala ti o lo kon ori'le
omo bibi.

Obara was naked, nudity knows no home, and it is the ant in one's house that bites one. Those were the Awos who made divination for the small red pepper when she went to fight the boundary war that started from the time of her ancestors that is, to procreate. She was told to make sacrifice with meat, crushed yam mixed with palm oil, rabbit and red cloth. She made the sacrifice.

When she started having children, Èsù clad them up with the red cloth with which she made sacrifice. When it comes out at divination, the person will be told that there is a woman close to him or her who is anxiously doing everything to have children. She will be advised to make sacrifice and will surely start having children.

They Also Made Divination for Awele, the Flirt:

They advised her to make sacrifice in order to avoid getting into trouble through her genitals. She refused to make the sacrifice and she continued with her flirtation. Meanwhile, she ensnared the son of the king to make love to her, which resulted in the death of the prince.

When the brothers and friends of the prince heard of the incident, they apprehended her and tied her up. She was paraded naked throughout the town and ended up at the palace. When the king asked her if she was given to making divination, she confirmed that she made divination but failed to make the recommended sacrifice, which is why she was punished with such harsh fate. The king ordered her release after putting the blame on his son who condescended to sex with a prostitute, and she regained her freedom to make the sacrifice.

At divination, the person will be told to beware of prostitution. For a woman, she should make sacrifice to avoid getting into trouble through sex. If the divinee is a man, he should beware of sleeping with prostitutes to avoid losing his life.

Chapter 5
Obara-Okonron

```
I I      I
I I     I I
I I     I I
 I      I I
```

Ebara Okonron wii. Adifa fun yeye igi ti a ni ko ru ebo tori fi abiku omo.

He made divination for the mother of trees, who was told to make sacrifice to avoid the danger of untimely death for her children. She was to make the sacrifice with an axe and a cutlass, but she refused to do it. That is why it is those same instruments that are used for felling her children (trees) to this day.

When the Odù appears at divination, the person should be advised to make sacrifice to obviate the danger of losing his or her children to the evil machinations of mankind.

He Made Divination for the Pounded Yam:

Ebara Okonron agogo ude ubale oro kanigo kanigo.
Ikpesi kagbo lorun jigi guo jigi guo. Agogo ude ko i
dun laye ki a gbo lo orun. Ikpesi koi dun laye ki a gbo
lo orun. Adifa fun Iyan onti kole orun bo wa si kole aye.
Òrúnmìlà ki iyan ru bo. Iyan koo ru ebo na.
Akiko ni ebo re kpelu aso fifun.

The brass gong fell down and sounded kanigo kanigo. The drum was beaten and it sounded jigi guo jigi guo. The sound of the brass gong on earth cannot be heard in heaven. The sound of the drumbeat on earth cannot be heard in heaven. These were the Awos who made divination for the pounded yam before it left heaven for earth. It was told to make sacrifice with cock, and white cloth but failed to do it. When it got to the world, it was subjected to the punishment of being beaten with pestle and mortar before taking shape and name.

When it appears at divination the person should be told to make sacrifice so that people might not team up to beat or kill him and to avoid loss of children.

He Made Divination for the Masquerade (Egungun):

Ebara gidi gba Awo Òrúnmìlà, Adifa fun Egungun onti'kole orun bo wa si kole aye.

The masquerade (Egungun) was told to make sacrifice for honor, prosperity and followership, before he left heaven. He made sacrifice with different clothes, cock, pigeon and hen.

When he appeared on earth, he was received with joy and respect, and people followed him about where ever he went. That is the situation to this day.

The Divination He Made Before Leaving Heaven:

Uruke mi lawo ligonrin, oroke mi la'wo leturuye, were the two Awos who made divination for Òrúnmìlà before he left heaven. He was advised to make sacrifice against the danger of unconsumated fortunes (Amubo in Yorùbá and Osobo no ma sunu in Bini). He was told to serve; Èsù with he-goat, Ifá with a goat, and Ògún with a dog. He made all the sacrifices before setting out for the world. His guardian angel persuaded Ògún to accompany him to the world and he agreed.

When he got to the world, he forgot that his prosperity was to depend on close cooperation with Ògún. Things did not move well with him. Although he was a practicing Ifá priest, he was neither recognized nor prosperous. He subsequently had a dream in which his guardian angel asked him why he has neglected Ògún and Èsù. The following morning, he consulted his Okekponrin and he was advised to serve; Èsù with a he-goat, Ògún with a dog; and his Ifá with a goat. He was to use the he-goat to wash the stigma of hard-luck on Èsù shrine. He performed all the sacrifices without any delay. He was told to give an ornamental brass scimitar and mitre to his Ifá.

Events soon brought him in close contact with the Oba. There was an outbreak of measles in the town caused by Èsù which caused a large toll in infant mortality. The more popular Awos were invited but they could not stop the spread of the epidemic. One night, the Oba had a dream in which Èsù told him to look for an Awo called Obara-Kanran, because he was the only one who could abate the measles epidemic.

The following morning, the Oba sent his royal messengers to scan the town for an Awo called Obara-Kanran, Towards midday, they succeeded in locating him. He was accordingly summoned to follow them to the palace, which he did without qualms. When he got to the palace, the Oba told him to divine on what had to be done to stop the spread of the ongoing measles epidemic. In the ensuing divination, he told the Oba to buy a three-year old he-goat for sacrifice to Èsù at once. He also disclosed that the calamity occurred because the Oba did not perform the Ògún festival for that year. He recommended that a dog, a cock, a tortoise, a snail, roasted yam and a gourd of palm wine should be used to serve Ògún immediately. He also revealed that the shrine of Shankpana at the main entrance to the town had been neglected for too long. It was to be served with a cock and fried corn. The sacrifices were made without delay.

Three days passed without any new cases of measles or child-death being reported. Before the end of seven days, the epidemic had abated, and the Oba compensated Obara-Okonron elaborately. He was subsequently given a chieftaincy title and made the chief royal diviner. The Oba caused a befitting house to be built for him. He had finally been translated into prosperity and eminence.

When this Odù appears at Ugbodu, the person should prepare his Ògún and Èsù shrines immediately.

At divination, the person should be told that he has not positioned his feet on the path of his destiny. He should have his own Ifá, Ògún and Èsù but must begin by giving he-goat to Èsù and dog to Ògún.

He Made Divination for the Rubbish Dump (Etitan in Yorùbá and Otiku in Bini):

Etitan was advised in heaven to serve Èsù with a he-goat and Ògún with a cock in order to avoid the danger of undulating fortunes. He was told to do the sacrifice so that after becoming prosperous, his fortunes might not ebb. He did not perform the sacrifice because he was sure that no day would pass without people sending gifts and food to him. He however served his guardian angel.

When he got to the world, he was doing very well because he continued to receive food and gifts on a daily basis. Meanwhile however, Èsù asked Ighoroko whether Etitan made sacrifice. He was told that he refused to make sacrifice. Èsù proceeded to incite Ògún to set the house of Etitan on fire. That deprived him of most of his belongings although he was still left with some remnants. That is why to this day, the rubbish dump is always set on fire from time to time when it is full, that is, at the height of its prosperity.

When this Odù appears at Ugbodu and at divination, the person should be told to serve Èsù with a he-goat and Ògún with a cock, to avoid the risk of undulating fortunes.

His Problems on Earth:

Obara-Okonron was a benevolent Ifá priest, a professional dancer, who performed magical feats in the process. One day he travelled to Oja Ajigbomekon for Ifá practice. Unknown to him, some enemies were plotting against him. A beneficiary of his magnanimity got wind of it and went to warn him not to spend the night in the place because there was a plot to assassinate him.

He decided to escape at dusk to the next town, but before leaving, he got the stem of plantain measured to his height and covered it up with his loin cloth on the bed on which he was supposed to sleep. When the assassins got to the room, they inflicted machete cuts on the bed and left. The following morning, when they went to verify the outcome of their despicable act, they were surprised to discover that it was a plantain stem they had butchered. They began to marvel that Obara-Okonron was indeed a strong Awo. His woes were however far from over.

In the new palace where he sought refuge, there was another plot to assassinate him. When he consulted Okeponrin, to seek new directions, Ifá advised him to serve Èsù with an infant he-goat and a missile (Akatapo in Yorùbá and Ekepede in Bini). After serving Èsù with the small he-goat, he butchered it on the shrine of Èsù and poured palm oil on it. Ifá assured him that those plotting against him would subsequently come to him to disclose their machinations.

Later that night, at the instance of Èsù, the Oloja of the town was suddenly taken ill and there was no other Awo to approach for help except Obara-Okonron who happened to be around. In desperation, the people decided to approach him. At divination, he declared that there was nothing to be done to save the Oloja's life because he was already slated to die. He added that after his death, six others would follow him to heaven. Asked what they could do to ameliorate the situation, he asked whether they were prepared to make sacrifice and they confirmed affirmatively. He told them to produce two hundred goats, two hundred hens and Two Hundred each of several other materials. Besides, he told them that if there was not to be famine in the town, the Oloja after becoming well should reveal the morbid plan they had made to kill a visiting Awo, because the town which kills an Ifá priest would know no peace.

The Oloja subsequently became well after the sacrifice was made. Thereafter he invited all the town's traditional diviners to cross-check the validity and veracity of the declarations made by the visiting Ifá priest. Meanwhile, Èsù went round to warn all the town's diviners that the town would experience a devastating catastrophe unless they removed the Oloja and replaced him with Obara-Okonron.

When the divine priests were assembled, the Ògún priest among them became possessed and while in trance, he proclaimed that the divine council had found the Oloja guilty of hatching a plan to kill a visiting Ifá priest, which was why he became critically ill. He added that the only salvation for the town was for the Oloja to step down and be replaced by the visiting Ifá priest. All the other diviners encored the declarations of the possessed Ògún priest.

A meeting of the town's elders was immediately convened and the changes were announced and Obara-Okonron was subsequently made the new Oloja, after the deposed Oloja made an open apology for his transgression.

When the Odù appears at Ugbodu, the person will be told to make sacrifice to Èsù and the Night because a position earmarked for him is in the offing. At divination the person should serve Èsù to frustrate the evil plans of his enemies.

He Made Divination for Prince Owolabi of Ijero:

Bi oju eni ba ti ri oran, Enu eni aa dake. Odifa fun
owolabi omo Ajero.

If one is suddenly confronted with danger, the mouth will be dumbfounded. That was the Awo who made divination for Owolabi, the son of the Ajero before he started a new farming year. He was advised to make sacrifice before embarking on the farm. He was to make a sacrifice with cutlass, cudgels and a he-goat. He refused to make the sacrifice. He insulted Èsù as Satan the thief and condemned the Ifá priest as an extortionate hoodlum, who went around trying to reap whatever he had not sown.

The following morning, he left home for the farm. As soon as he got to the farm a heavy rain started falling. It did not rain for long. When the rain subsided, Owolabi started planting his crops. Among the crops he planted was sugar cane. It was subsequently the first to produce a prolific harvest. When the sugar cane was ripe for harvesting, Owolabi sent his young son to go and cut from the sugar cane in the farm. As the boy was about to cut the sugar cane, he saw a human skull which had been positioned there by Èsù. The boy was gripped with fear when the skull asked him whether he was going to cut the sugar cane. Before he could reply, the skull told him to inform his father that a heavy rain was going to fall at the Ajero's palace. The boy took to his heels and ran home, thoroughly frightened.

On getting home, he narrated his strange experience to his father, who instead of believing his story, admonished him for not returning home with the sugar cane. The father asked him whether he had ever seen a corpse, and the boy did not know what to say. To test the veracity of his story, the father decided to follow him to the farm. On getting there he saw no sign of the skull which the boy spoke about. The father became so paranoid that he beheaded his son. As soon as the dead boy fell to the ground, the mysterious skull reappeared on top of the sugar cane plant, exclaiming "Ha! ha! ha! so you beheaded you son as if you were chopping off a plantain". When Owolabi heard the words of the skull, her ran home to tell the people that the story of the skull was true because it had spoken to him.

The people followed him to the farm, but saw no talking skull, except the corpse of his dead son. He was accused of faking the story to cover up the murder of his son. In the ensuing scuffle, one of the people beheaded him. The head chopping cycle continued until there were seven corpses on the ground. The eighth person ran home to the palace to tell the Ajero what had happened at Owolabi's farm.

The Oba sent some people to go and verify the story. When they got to the farm, the verifiers were in the process of accusing the informant of murdering the dead persons, when the skull reemerged to declare the informant's innocence, adding that "there was going to be a heavy rain at the palace of the Ajero, because of the sacrifice that Owolabi failed to make. That was the story carried home by the verifiers to the Ajero, who invited his Ifá priests to divine and make the prescribed sacrifices.

That is why when this Odù appears at divination, the person will be told not to eat sugar cane and to make sacrifice to avoid the danger of committing murder.

Chapter 6
Obara-Irosun

```
   I      I
   I     I I
  I I    I I
  I I    I I
```

Made Divination for the Children of Prosperity Before They Left Heaven:

Ebara kosun sose osi oda ose otun si, oda fun omo ati aya ati aje ati gbogbo ure, nijo ti won ti kole lo wa si kole aye. Ani ki won ru ebo.

Ebara rubbed camwood (red chalk) on his two legs when he made divination for the children of prosperity; childbirth, marriage, money, position, and all items of wealth, when they were leaving heaven for earth. They were told to make sacrifice so that they might become precious assets to be sought after by all and sundry. Money was told to make sacrifice with pigeon, Marriage to make sacrifice with a he-goat, Childbirth was to make sacrifice with a hen, and Elevation was to make sacrifice with a ram. They all made the sacrifices before leaving heaven. The moment they got to the world, they became the dream and aspiration of kings and commoners alike.

When it appears at Ugbodu, the person will be told to make sacrifice for him to become immensely prosperous.

Òrúnmìlà Declares the Sacrifice for Opening the Gates to Prosperity:

Òrúnmìlà ni ki olu shiku; Emi ki alaworo shiku.
Òrúnmìlà ni ki ni olu yio fi shiku. Emi na ni kini
alaworo yio fi shiku. Ayebo adiye; Eyele, ugbin,
eku, eja, eko, akara, ekpo ati obi.

Òrúnmìlà told the gatekeeper to open. I told Òrúnmìlà to ask the divine priest to open the door. I asked Òrúnmìlà how the gatekeeper was going to open it, and Òrúnmìlà asked how the divine priest was going to open the door.

He said that the gate was going to be opened with a hen, pigeon, snail, rat, fish, eko, akara and kolanuts.

The materials were produced and the gate to the house of treasure was opened. This is the special sacrifice (Ono-Ifá or Odiha) of this Odù at Ugbodu.

He Made Divination for the Woman Who Had Six Children:

Ebara gosun gosun, oshowo udo poro poro. Adifa fun yeye olomo mefa mati'yo. Ebo ni koru to ri iku omo. Ebara rubbed camwood and washed his hands inside the mortar. He made divination for the mother of six children. She was told to make sacrifice against the danger of losing any of her children to death. She made the sacrifice with he-goat, cock and pigeon.

When it appears at divination, the person will be advised to make sacrifice to obviate the danger of losing children as he or she gets older.

He Made Divination for a Mother Having Two Daughters:

A woman had two daughters who were always going to battle as soldiers. Before going to war, the eldest daughter used to position an egg on top of a stone, while the junior one kept her one egg on top of the cover of a calabash plate. They often left instructions with their mother that if the eggs fell to the ground, it would mean that they had been killed in battle.

On one occasion before they went to the battle of Oshen, they went for divination and they were told to give he-goat to Èsù before going. They only gave the skulls of he-goat and chickens to Èsù, promising to give live he-goats, if they returned safely from the war. Long after they left for the war, their mother observed one morning that the two eggs and fallen to the ground and broken to pieces. Their opponents had given them cock and bitter leaf, which they forbade, thus neutralizing their powers. On seeing the position of the eggs, their mother immediately concluded that the war had consumed her two daughters. She reacted by running to River Aiye to collect it's sand. Traditionally, no one looked at the sand from that river because anyone who saw, it died immediately. She removed the sand, covered it up in a plate and left with the plate for the battle front at Oshen.

On getting to Oshen she made enquiries about the fate of two young girls who came to participate in the battle for the town. They told her that their fate was a forgotten issue because they had long been killed on the Ògún and Uja shrines. With the bad news, she immediately opened the plate of sand and all those who saw it were falling to their deaths. She had killed many people in the town before getting to the palace of the king of Oshen, who ran away from his throne. She pursued the king and as she was about to catch up with him, he transfigured into a hillock and the woman turned into a beehive to surround the hillock.

When this Odù appears at Ugbodu, the person will be told that a war is imminent for him. He should give a he-goat to Èsù to survive it. He should be advised to forbid bitterleaf and the meat of any male bird including cock and drake. At divination the person should be told to serve Èsù and to refrain from accompanying anyone on a journey. He should also offer sacrifice to the water divinity.

The Divination Made for Him Before He Left Heaven:

Oshupa ko le she ko ma ton lo sho-shu. Orun ko le ja bo laye e. Adifa fun Òrúnmìlà ni jo to'n ti kole orun bo wa si kole aye.

The moon never fails to appear every month and the sun never falls from its orbit from rising till setting. These were the two Awos who made divination for Òrúnmìlà when he was leaving heaven for the earth. He was told to make sacrifice to avoid having difficulties during his life on earth. He was told to; serve Èsù with a he-goat, adding white and red cloths, serve ifa with a dove (Adaba in Yorùbá of Idu in Bini), and to give cock to Sàngó. He made the sacrifices.

On getting to the world, he had initial difficulties. He could not afford to marry, and so had no child and no house of his own. When he subsequently went for divination, he was advised to prepare his own Sàngó with a cock and his own Ògún with a tortoise and a cock. He was also told to give a he-goat to Èsù and a dove to his Ifá. He again did the sacrifices.

After the sacrifice, he began to thrive in his work and began to prosper. He was able to have a wife, bear children (and children) and subsequently built his own house. Ògún and Sàngó began to assist him in many ways.

When this Odù appears at Ugbodu, the person should prepare his own Ògún and Sàngó, in addition to putting a thunder stone on his Ifá shrine.

The Dishonesty of His Servants:

He had as three servants; the Elephant, the Parrot and the Dog. When he went on tour for Ifá practice, the Elephant stole his divination tray (Akpako) and wore it round his neck. He also stole his uranke (divination staff) and kept it in his mouth. The Dog swallowed up his ASE while the Parrot removed the red Aluko feathers with which he decorated his Ifá shrine.

When he discovered the theft upon his return from tour, he consulted Ifá on what to do to recover what his dishonest servants had stolen. He was told to serve Ògún with a tortoise and a cock, which he did. Ògún then turned to a hunter and shot down the Elephant to remove the uranke (tusks) and the parrot to remove the red feathers. The Dog however became elusive, but when Ògún wanted to perform his annual festival he apprehended the Dog and used him for sacrifice but could not recover the ASE which he had swallowed.

Òrúnmìlà Laments the Unreliability of Human Nature:

Òrúnmìlà wipe Õbara lu-rosun.
Moni eni re-re ni a ri ba jaiye.
Oni ta ni eni rere ti a ri ba j'aiye?
Moni Ògún oni jan-o-le, ejemu olu won ronwi aja gidigidi i-gba-sa
Òrúnmìlà ni kiin she Ògún ni eni rere ti a ri ba j'aiye.
Òrúnmìlà ni Obara-lu-ro-sun.
Moni eni rere ni a ri ba j'aiye.
Oni ta ni eni rere ti a ri ba j'aiye?
Moni Olota ni Ado.
Moni ren-rin ni Owo
Moni ose eni ilu Magbon.
Moni ugba erumole ti o nta'la.
Òrúnmìlà ni awon won yi ni.
Won ni ki n she eni rere ti a le ri ba j'aiye?

In a dialogue with his follower,
Òrúnmìlà said Obara prostrated.
I replied that it was a nice person that one could enjoy life with.
Òrúnmìlà asked, who is the good person that one can find to enjoy life with?
I said it is Ògún, but Òrúnmìlà rejected Ògún.
I suggested Olota at Adu, Rin-rin at Owo or Ose of Imagbon.
Òrúnmìlà kept quiet.
Then I suggested the Two Hundred Divinities as suitable associates to enjoy life with,
but he again rejected them.
I then asked Òrúnmìlà for the ideal person.
He finally replied that it is only one's head and one's guardian angel who
do not mislead or deceive one on earth.

The priest then asked Òrúnmìlà for the sacrifice, and he replied that it required pounded yam with Egusi soup prepared with oily fish. That is why Òrúnmìlà sings:-

Oro yi ko kan Ògún, osi kan Orisa
Oro yi kò kan Ògún, osi kan Orisa
eleda eni ni oro yi kan

The matter does not affect Ògún, or Orisa.
It only refers to one's guardian angel.

At divination, the person should be advised to have his own Ifá and to serve his head with a Guinea-fowl in order to prosper in life.

Chapter 7
Obara-Owanrin
Obara-Lila

```
I I    I
I I    I I
I      I I
I      I I
```

The Divination Made for Him Before Leaving Heaven:

Ebun ofe kii je ra lowo eyan,
Ore olo're ni mo ma fi'la.
Awon l'ondifa fun Òrúnmìlà ni jo ti o kole orun si bo wa kole aye.

A free gift does not forebode danger in the hands of the recipient. I will prosper through the fortunes of other people. These were the two Awos who made divination for Obara-Lila when he was leaving heaven for the world. He was advised to serve; Ifá with a goat, Èsù with he-goat, and his mother with a hen, including all cooking condiments. He made all the sacrifices and left for the world, after obtaining clearance from his guardian angel.

On getting to the world, he became a trader and a farmer. His early success evoked enmity and his relations began to create problems for him. His business took a downturn in fortune and he decided to go for divination. He was told to serve; his Ifá with a goat, Èsù with a he-goat and to serve his mothers head with a hen. His own Ifá priest made the sacrifices for him and he was assured that fortune awaited him in his business.

One day a group of bandits hid their loot near his farm. When he subsequently got to his farm, he saw the loot comprising several items of treasure, bags of clothes, beads, elephant tusks, money, eagle's and parrot's feathers. He left the materials on the first day without touching them. When he got home he consulted Ifá who told him that the bandits who kept the treasures near his farm had been caught and executed. It was the following day that he removed the materials to his house. The finds made him very wealthy and he went to express his gratitude to the Ifá priests by giving them a bag of money, a goat and pieces of cloths. Meanwhile, Ifá had told him that he was yet to collect another loot.

He used to trade to Oja-Ajigbomekon Akira. When he got to the market one day, he saw a number of elephant tusks and other precious wares at his stall. He was later told that a robber had been apprehended that morning. When the market dispersed, no one came to claim the goods. Once again, he enquired from Ifá who cleared him to go home with them. With that, his wealth multiplied and his prosperity assumed superlative proportions. Once more, he went to thank the Awos who made divination and sacrifice for him by giving each of them one elephant's tusks, a piece of white cloth and a bag of money. Thus, his destiny manifested by indirectly benefiting through the fortunes of others from his farming as well as his trading.

When this Ifá appears at Ugbodu, the person should be told that his fortune will come from farming (especially in yams and maize) and trading. He will be enriched legitimately by the fortunes of other people. He should keep elephant's tusks on his Ifá shrine. At divination, the person should be told to have his own Ifá, if a man, or to marry an Ifá man, if a woman.

He Becomes a High Chief of His Town:

Meanwhile, the Oba of his town soon began to hear about his wealth and popularity. One day the Oba invited him for divination and he said he was not a practicing Ifá priest. The king had kept three containers in his private room containing, a piece of chalk, cowries and alligator pepper. He told him to name the contents of each of the three containers. He went home to prepare for the test.

Èsù immediately transfigured into a girl selling little articles and gave him a chalk, a cowry and an alligator pepper. When he got home, he enquired from Ifá the significance of the gifts given to him by the girl, and Ifá confirmed that they were the contents of the three containers kept by the king in his private room. He was holding the three materials when he got to the palace and told the king what the three containers contained. The Oba then asked him why he declined to be practicing Ifá priest, and he replied that he was not destined to be one. He was instantly made the Shasere of the town with a plea from the Oba to help him to administer the kingdom.

Divination for Òrúnmìlà on Caution:

Ebara wonrin koso ni she owo imole. Adifa fun Òrúnmìlà ni jo ti baba maashe owo imola laa.

That was the Awo who made divination for Òrúnmìlà when he was advised to act with caution and never to do things in a hurry. He was told to make sacrifice with a pigeon and the knife used for circumcision, (Obeke in Yorùbá and Abe-Osiwu in Bini) and a forkstick. The sacrifice was made and the knife and forkstick were prepared for him to hold when travelling.

One day, as he was roving in the forest, he came across a kolanut tree whose fruits were ripe for plucking. The owners of the tree had no equipment for plucking the kolanuts. He gave them his forkstick which they used to pluck all the kolanuts. Later, he also gave them his knife to use for splitting the fruits. After preparing the kolanuts, they divided it into three parts and gave him one part. He transported his share of the kolanuts home and sold them for good money.

Made Divination for the Man Who Caught a Treasure Bird:

Ebara wonrin ayoro ima, ayoro ima, idowo okpe meji. Kooyo ko ga jura won lo. Adafa fun ashan esin suni gba ojo tonlo roko roko ton lo gbe eye oda wa le.

He made divination for the man who was clearing the road when it was raining. At the end of the exercise, and following the sacrifice he had made, he caught a bird that was capable of bringing prosperity to its owner. The bird made him to become very wealthy.

He Made Divination for the Hunter:

A hunter had three dogs which he had trained to help him in a variety of ways including hunting. The dogs were called; Ugbo ngbo lo ju ode, Amomimau and Ajorijawe. When he went for divination, he was told to make sacrifice to avoid problems from his hunting. He was at that time proposing to go on tour, so he decided he would perform the sacrifice upon his return from tour.

While he was away on tour, his wife went hunting with the dogs without knowing how the husband used to treat them. Since she did not know how to feed them, the three dogs died. Following the death of the dogs, she contrived a new strategy for raising money. She arranged with a parrot to climb an oak tree on the way to the market to be making divination from there. When people saw her receiving instructions from the oak tree, they followed her example and she was able to collect a large sum of money in the process.

When the operation was over, she collected all the money alone without giving the parrot any share of it. The parrot reacted by going to live with her, refusing to leave until he got his share. That was the state of affairs when her husband returned home. Before returning home, the rumor was already circulating in the town that she was cohabiting with the parrot. As the woman was unable to put up a satisfactory explanation for the demise of the dogs and the presence of the parrot in the house, the husband drove her out of his house while he kept the parrot to be assisting him as an informant.

When this Ifá appears at Ugbodu, the person will be advised to serve Èsù with a he-goat and Ifá with two hens to obviate the risk of being involved in a dispute over money. He should also rear a dog. At divination, the person should offer he-goat to Èsù because of some money he would be asked to come and collect.

He Made Divination for Olobara:

Òrúnmìlà ni ishe-she, moni ishe she.
Ishe-she erin, erin di ara igbo.
Iya je efon, o di ero odan.
Iya je ipale oro kan, o di eni a ngun fun ewure.
Adafa fun Olobara ti o lo san iyan alai l'obe yo.

Òrúnmìlà says abject penury. I said abject penury.
It was abject penury that turned the elephant
into a forest animal.
It was as a punishment that the buffalo became a wild
open-field grazing animal.
It was the punishment from offensive words that made a
man to ride on a goat.

These were the Awos who made divination for Olobara who had to eat pounded yam without soup. He was advised to make sacrifice so that he would always eat pounded yam with soup. In other words he was to make sacrifice so that his sufferings in the morning will end with the joy of opulence in the evening of his life. He was told to make the sacrifice with pigeon and cock. He made the sacrifice after which he was able to marry, have children, servants and to build houses. He became so prosperous that whenever he called one person, several persons would answer him.

When the Odù appears at divination, the person will be told to offer sacrifice to the Ifá in his family, so that his sufferings will change to joy and prosperity.

Chapter 8
Obara-Ogunda

```
I    I
I    I I
I    I I
I I  I I
```

He Made Divination for Deyi, the Livestock Farmer:

Obara-Ogunda was invited to take care of Deyi, the livestock farmer, when he was very ill. When he got to Deyi's house, it was too late to embark on divination. He therefore promised to do divination the following morning. The town was mainly inhabited by women.

Later on that night, the town's cult of witchcraft sent some witches to visit him. When they asked him what he came to do, he disclosed that he was invited to come and find out what made Deyi to become ill and why the sickness was not responding to treatment. The witches told Obara-Ogunda that the man was ill because of his stinginess. They informed him that although he was making huge profits in his livestock business, he did not consider it necessary to make any sacrifice whatsoever. They advised him that if he wanted Deyi to become well, he should ask him to make sacrifice to the night with two each of his birds and animals.

When Obara-Ogunda subsequently made divination in the morning, he told Deyi that he would only become well if he made sacrifice with two each of his different birds and animals. His host bluntly refused to make the sacrifice. In anger, Obara-Ogunda returned home without doing anything more for Deyi.

Subsequently, Deyi became well, and resumed his business. One day before he returned from the market, all his birds and animals went into his room and removed his clothes and ran with them into the forest. As they were leaving, they began to sing:-

Ija bele ta ko ko,
Eran abule egbedo kpa sibe,
Eran gbule egbedo kpa si le,
Ija bele bele ta ko ko.

When he returned to discover what had happened, he quickly sent for Obara-Ogunda. He eventually made the sacrifice and his life was saved, but he had lost his livestock.

When this Odù appears at Ugbodu, the person should use a goat to make sacrifice at his ancestral shrine, serve Ògún with a dog, and give a goat to the night. At divination, the person should be advised to give a he-goat to Èsù and a cock to Ògún.

Made Divination for Agbe and Onne:

Agbe marari, Onne waka wa ka mararu ugban. Adifa fun Agbe
tinshe ore Onne, atun dafun Onne ti nshe ore Agbe ni jo ti awon
meje ji nshe ore arawon.

The bird called Agbe in Yorùbá or Awe in Bini was befriending the crocodile (Onne). Agbe and Onne went for divination and they were both advised to make sacrifice. Agbe was to make sacrifice with a Guinea-fowl and Onne was to make sacrifice with a he-goat and divination tray (Akpako). They made the sacrifices. Onne complained to Agbe that human beings were after him and sought his assistance. Agbe reassured him that he would always give him a warning signal whenever his human enemies were on his trail to attack him.

Not long afterwards, men came with instruments for capturing Onne. As soon as Agbe saw them, he began to sing: Onne waka waka, gbe kpakoru (several times). When Onne heard the warning, he dived into the water covering his head with the Akpako prepared for him following the sacrifice he made. No matter the poison which the hunters threw into the water, it did not affect Onne. That was how he developed his survival strategy.

At divination the person should be told to serve Èsù with a he-goat including the bone of crocodile and the red feather of Agbe in order to survive the evil machinations of his enemies.

He Made Divination for Gberesi Before She Got Married:

Okiti bamba ni Kpeku okpokpo. Odifa fun gberesi ti o bi ni
eka awunsi, to tun lo ni oko lo'ode ominikun.

That was the Awo who made divination for a girl called Gberesi of the town of Eka-Awunsi when she was going to marry a husband in the town of Ominikun. She was told to make sacrifice with a he-goat and a cock in order to enjoy a successful marriage. She made the sacrifice and the Awo prepared leaves for her to bath. The marriage brought her eternal happiness in several ways.

If this Odù appears for a man, he will be told that a woman is coming to marry him and that whenever she comes, he should invite Awos to prepare leaves for her to bath, because she is Òrúnmìlà's wife (Akpetebi). If she does not already have Ifá, he should be told to arrange to have it. Meanwhile, he should make sacrifice with a hen and a he-goat.

He Made Divination for Sixteen Witches:

Asa mu irin ko. Ajawara wara mu ikako.
Ari ikin gbe jo ni o se Awo isa'laye.
Ajawara wara mu ida ko ni ose ode-orun.
Ami-mi-sa-sa, ni odifa fun Ajé merindilogun
l'ojo ti won o lo ti enu ije gbo ohun.

Those were the four Awos who made divination for Sixteen Witches when they were trying to find out the secret of prosperity from Òrúnmìlà.

Òrúnmìlà told them that those who wished to know the secrets of life should listen to the chants on the divination tray. Those who desire to have money, marriage, children, must appeal to divination and sacrifice, being the roots of prosperity.

The witches listened to the poem on prosperity and they went away happy and satisfied.

When this Odù appears at divination, the person will be advised to take his problems to Ifá and whatever he or she is told by Òrúnmìlà will truly manifest.

He Made Divination for the Oba and the People of Idanren:

When Obara-Ogunrere was leaving heaven, he was advised to make sacrifice to Ifá with a goat and Ifá knife (Aza) and to give he-goat to Èsù. He was told to make the sacrifice so as to live long on earth, and he did. He became a famous Ifá priest on earth and subsequently travelled to the land of Idanren where he made divination for the Oba.

He told the Oba that they never used to live long in his family, and that it was time to change the misfortune. He told the Oba to make sacrifice with a goat, a he-goat, a dog and an Ifá knife. He told the Oba that from then on he was not to touch the ground with his head for any other divinity apart from his own Ifá.

After the departure of Obara-Ogunda, some people who went about praying in white apparels visited the town and convinced the Oba to abandon the worship of any other divinity apart from their foreign god. He subsequently abandoned his ancestral divinities and Òrúnmìlà. Things soon became difficult for him. His subjects rebelled against him for abandoning all their traditional rites and rituals. He eventually sent for Obara-Ogunda who blamed him for fouling himself with the worship of a strange divinity. He was able to refurbish himself after making sacrifice with a ram and two pigeons. After the sacrifice, his subjects resumed the payment of homage and respects to him.

When this Odù appears at Ugbodu, the person should be told to refrain from touching the ground with his head for any other divinity, apart from Òrúnmìlà. The person should be forewarned against the time he would abandon his Ifá and turn to Christianity. If he throws away his Ifá, he will be forced to have it rehabilitated when between the devil and the deep blue sea.

Chapter 9
Obara-Osa

```
I I    I
I      I I
I      I I
I      I I
```

The Sacrifice He Made Before Running Away From Heaven:

This Odù ran away from heaven. It was his own guardian angel that advised him to make sacrifice before he ran away from heaven. He was told to serve his head with a cock and to give a Guinea-fowl to his guardian angel. He also gave a he-goat to Èsù and served the ground of heaven with a tortoise.

Thereafter, he left for earth without telling anybody. On getting to the world he took to trading which took him to several places. He was always travelling about and around. When he discovered that he was making no head way, he went for divination and he was told to practice Ifism in addition to his trading. Once again, he served; his Ifá with a Guinea-fowl, his head with a Guinea-fowl, because he forbade cock, Èsù with a he-goat and the ground with a tortoise. As he began to operate as an Ifá priest, he found himself inching into prosperity. People soon observed that he was more proficient as an Ifá priest than as a trader. As he began to prosper, he settled down to a more homely life.

When this Odù appears at Ugbodu, the person should be told to take to business as his main profession, but should also learn how to read Ifá. He should resist the temptation to travel too often away from home.

His Encounter With the Cult of Witchcraft:

When he was busy travelling about, he has no time for his family. When his son Sheyi grew up, he gave him out to Sàngó to live with him as a servant. Sàngó used to hold meetings in heaven and any time he could not go, he often sent Sheyi to represent him. Sàngó had two other servants. One was a hunter while the other was a repairer with the capability to restore all damaged or defective objects.

Once upon a time, there was famine on earth because there was no rain throughout the rainy season. The people of the earth went to enquire from Sàngó why there had been no rain, since he used to communicate with heaven. He agreed to find out on his next trip to heaven.

At a subsequent meeting of the divine council in heaven, Sàngó was told that the Cult of Witchcraft (Awon-Iyami Osoronga) had laid three eggs on the sky which had the effect of holding up the rain from falling. God explained that if He became angry, the eggs would break and there would be chaos. The council told Sàngó that if it was possible to find someone who could empty the contents of one of the eggs and return the empty shell in place, there would be rain within three days.

When Sàngó returned to earth, he asked his hunter/servant whether he would be able to shoot one of the eggs without disturbing the other two. The hunter wore his hunting costume and used his weapon to take aim. He shot the egg and it fell to the ground without breaking. The repairer was invited to open the egg and empty its content into Obara-Osa's Oriole, the shrine of the Ground Divinity. Thereafter, he pieced the shell together and Sheyi, who used to go to heaven agreed to return the empty egg shell in place and he did so. The Cult of Witchcraft did not know what was happening because the events transpired by daytime.

When night came, the witches discovered that one of their eggs was empty. They reacted by delivering a message from heaven that the Divinity of Death was ill and they wanted earthly Awos volunteer to come to heaven to cure him. They added a rider that if on the other hand, the contents of their egg could be found, the divinity of Death would get well. Everyone concluded that Obara-Osa was the only Awo who could cure the divinity of Death. When he consulted his Okeponrin, he discovered that there was nothing wrong with Death and that the elders of the night were merely looking for a sacrificial victim. It was at that stage that Obara-Osa decided to give the cult of witchcraft the fight of their life.

That night, he went outside his house with his divination tray in hand carrying the markings of Osameji and Ose-ogbe on it, and began to say:-

Ugbane gun Ugbanero.
Ugbane Kpurughu rughu.
Arufen Ana le leke.

When the witches challenged him that he was the one keeping the contents of their egg, he retorted that he could not have held the contents of their egg when he did not go to heaven. He then poured the contents of the divination tray into his Oriole. Thereafter, the witches told him that they came to arrest him. He however told them that they could not arrest him. When they were about to start a fight, he invited them to enjoy a meal of snails before combat. As soon as they finished eating, all the witches fell asleep and for the first time in a year, the rain began to fall. The witches slept till the following morning and it rained throughout the night. There was general rejoicing all over the earth.

When this Odù appears at Ugbodu, the person should immediately offer sacrifice to the Night. He should be advised never to keep a servant. If his mother is still alive, he should buy her a hen with which to serve her head. If she is late, he should serve his head with a hen and fish. At divination, the person should serve; his head with a cock, and Ògún with another cock. He should not keep a servant.

Made Divination for the Father of Ojulewa:

Tolo Tolo abi eru ba sa, bi omo ba saa, a o basa. Adafa fun aye to on wa Ojulewa omo re kiri ode. Ebo ni koru, ko le ri Ojulewa.

When a slave escapes, the owner will look for him. When a child is missing, the parents will also search for him. These were the Awos who made divination for the father of Ojulewa when she ran away from home. He was told to make sacrifice with a he-goat and he did. He subsequently found the girl.

He Made Divination for Òrúnmìlà to Become Victorious at War:

Aya korigi korigi efon, adifa fun Òrúnmìlà ni jo ti onlo si Ògún aja gberin osheshe.

That was the name of the Awo, with a heart as strong as that of buffalo, who made divination for Òrúnmìlà when he embarked on a war in which he was victorious. He was advised to make sacrifice with a he-goat, rabbit, and palm oil, and he did it. He then left for the war front with the other one hundred and ninety nine divinities. Ifá had advised Òrúnmìlà not to leave for the war front with the others but to allow them to precede him.

When the rest got to the war front, they fought hard under the command of Ògún, and each of them captured four hundred prisoners. As they were returning, Èsù advised Òrúnmìlà to meet them on the way. Òrúnmìlà met Ògún first and congratulated him, adding that he was just coming to play his part. Thereafter, he planted the red feathers of Aluko on the head of Ògún to decorate him to mark his victory. In appreciation, Ògún gave Òrúnmìlà one hundred war captives. Next, he met Òrìsà-Nlá and congratulated him by decorating his head with two parrot's feathers, in return for which he got one hundred war captives. He also met Olókun who after being congratulated and decorated, gave him one hundred war captives. When he met Olofin, he gave him Iyere Okin, the feathers of the king of birds, which the Oba used to decorate his crown. In return Olofin gave him two hundred war captives. His tote made him the most prolific beneficiary of a war in which he did not physically participate.

Divination for Long Life and Prosperity:

    Òrúnmìlà ni ki Obara-Osa koko.
    Emi niki Obara-Osa ke-ke.
    Oni bi Olobara bati nsa koko, ti o si nsa.
    Ke-ke ni eni ma n ni aje.
    Òrúnmìlà niki Obara-osa ko-ko.
    Moni ki Olobara sa ke-ke
    Nigbati Olobara ba ti nsa ko-ko ti o ba ti nsa keke,
    Gbogbo ire ni o nwo ile.

    Òrúnmìlà told Obara-Osa to chant the tune.
    I told Obara-Osa to repeat the tune.

Òrúnmìlà explained that whenever Obara-Osa chants his tune repeatedly for anybody, the more prosperous the person becomes, and good fortune will move into the house. I asked Òrúnmìlà for the requisite sacrifice, and he recommended that we should use pigeon for wealth, cock for marriage, rat and a hen just beginning to lay eggs for children, a goat for filling the house with prosperity, a ram for upliftment, and a sheep for longevity.

When the sacrifice is made, prosperity must surely follow, because; the pigeon uses its two wings to fly wealth into the house, the cock does not present wine and yams before taking a wife, the rabbit never comes to the world without having children, the hen does not suffer from labor pains, the house is full (Ilekun-ke-ke) is the traditional cry of the goat, a three-year-old ram suffers no insult before getting a crown, an old sheep having white hairs all over its body, are its grey hairs, and "I will live long (temipe-temipe) is the customary cry of the sheep when it is on a hard ground.

At divination the person should make sacrifice with all the materials mentioned above in order to enjoy long life and prosperity.

Chapter 10
Obara-Etura

```
 I      I
I I    I I
 I     I I
 I     I I
```

He made divination for the Head:

Awo ori, odifa fun Ori tonwa aye apesin.

This Odù made divination for the Head when he was coming to a life in which he was to be universally served by all and sundry. He made sacrifice with a goat, a bell and a piece of white cloth. That is why all divinities and mortals alike, serve the head to the present day.

He Also Made Divination for the Trumpet (Ukpe):

Ebara Tua Tua Tua, Awo ukpe, odifa ukpe nijo ti o fe lo mu ale ibudo.

He made divination for the Trumpet when he was yearning for recognition. He was told to make sacrifice with a cock and a knife. Thereafter, he was told to go to the farm and stay by the young palm tree (Okpe-kete in Yorùbá and Okhere in Bini). When it germinated, it climbed to all the branches of the young palm tree and had many children. Èsù subsequently went to Olofin and taught him how to use Ukpe as the trumpet for his annual festival. Èsù went to the farm and blew the trumpet and everybody at home heard the sound. He then came to blow it at home and everybody in the farm, forest, market etc., heard the sound. The Oba was impressed so much that he decreed that henceforth, the trumpet would constitute the clarion call for inviting people for the worship of Ògún, and for calling people to arms in the event of a war. That was how Ukpe became very famous.

When it appears at divination the person should be told to make sacrifice because he was destined to become an indispensable personality in his community.

He Made Divination for Three Brothers:

Alagbara (Ògún) Oloogun (Òsanyìn) and Otito (Òrúnmìlà) were three brothers who left heaven for earth at the same time. When they went for divination, they were told to serve Èsù with he-goat in order to succeed in whatever they were going to do on earth. They were also advised to feast their guardian angels with a goat, and to obtain clearance from God with white cloth, white pigeon, white chalk and red parrot's feathers. Ògún and Òsanyìn did not bother to do the sacrifices, but Òrúnmìlà did all of them. Nonetheless, they all came to the world.

Each of them succeeded in building his own house. One day, the three of them travelled to Ife for Awo practice. At Ife, Òrúnmìlà was in the habit of dressing up in white apparel every morning and sitting in front of the house. Òrúnmìlà relied on telling the truth, Ògún relied on his physical strength, while Òsanyìn relied on his diabolical powers.

Meanwhile, the wife of the Olofin had been in labor for seven days and could not deliver. Òsanyìn, the physician, was the first to be invited to help. He used all the medicines he knew but could not make the woman deliver.Ògún was also invited but try as he did, he could not make her deliver the child. That was the point at which Èsù influenced the royal adviser to propose to Olofin to invite the man who used to dress in white clothes.

Two messengers were subsequently sent to invite Òrúnmìlà. He followed then to the palace where he immediately embarked on divination. After divination, he declared that the reason the woman could not deliver was because she had cohabited adulterously with three different men. He added that if she confessed and mentioned their names, she would presently deliver. When the woman was told about the declaration of Òrúnmìlà, she admitted it and mentioned the names of the men. Almost immediately afterwards, she gave birth to a male child. There was general rejoicing thereafter.

The Oba expressed his appreciation with elaborate gifts to Òrúnmìlà. It was following that incident that people realized what Òrúnmìlà was capable of doing. Clients soon began to rush to him for divination, from which he realized a lot of money. Not long afterwards, he was able to build a house at Ife.

On the other hand, neither Ògún nor Òsanyìn was able to make it. When they went for divination, they were told to return to the land of their birth to make sacrifice. They subsequently returned home to make sacrifice. They however delivered a message to Òrúnmìlà that he was required to return home to be made Oba. Òrúnmìlà eventually returned home to take the crown while Ògún and Òsanyìn after their sacrifices, began to prosper at Ife.

When this Ifá appears at Ugbodu, the person should be told to make sacrifice because a high position or chieftaincy title awaits him in the land of his birth.

Divined for Òrúnmìlà When His Farm Was Being Plundered:

The Porcupine (Ighogho in Yorùbá and Osorhue in Bini) and the grass-cutter (Ure in Yorùbá and Okhaen in Bini), were eating from the farm of Obara-Etura and he did not mind because he was very generous. Not satisfied with eating from the farm, the two rodents began to destroy the crops in the farm. It was a wine tapper who eventually reported the incident to Òrúnmìlà. He then sent a stern warning to the two heartless plunderers to stop eating grains in his farm.

They reacted by inviting the elephant and the pig to feed on and destroy the farm. The palm wine tapper saw the two big animals destroying the farm. After laying the farm bare, they waited for Òrúnmìlà to show up. The palm wine tapper went and told Òrúnmìlà what was happening but warned him not to go to the farm. The weaver bird and his friend Moteye the whistler also warned Òrúnmìlà not to go to the farm. When he consulted Ifá, he was told to give he-goat to Èsù and cock to Ògún but not to go to the farm because the ungrateful beneficiaries of his benevolence had plotted death for him. He however appealed to Èsù and Ògún to wage war on the enemies.

After enjoying their food, Èsù and Ògún directed the hunter to go to Òrúnmìlà's farm where he saw the elephant and the pig and shot them, dead. Èsù also pushed the porcupine and the grass-cutter to enter the traps and both of them died. That was how Òrúnmìlà got rid of his ungrateful enemies.

When this Ifá appears at Ugbodu, the person should be told that although he is benevolent, people are prone to returning his good turn with ingratitude. The people for whom he does favors will always turn round to try to kill him. He should give he-goat to Èsù, cock to Ògún to fight his enemies for him. At divination, the person should serve Èsù won account of an impending contest and favor. He should avoid a light complexioned woman.

He Made Divination for the People of Aiyetoro:

He made divination when he was invited by the people of Aiyetoro when they were threatened by war. He was told to make sacrifice with Eye Agbe (a bird) a cock, a knife and plenty of cold water so that he might accomplish his task and earn respect and praise. He made the sacrifice and left for Aiyetoro.

When he got there, he made divination and advised the people to make sacrifice with a pig, plenty of snails and a whistle. The made the sacrifice at a time when the town was already surrounded by enemy troops.

After the sacrifice, Èsù took the whistle and began to blow it round the town. Crying "moti se bo obara tua tua tua." While still blowing the whistle, Èsù sent his friend to warn the enemy troops that if they saw the person blowing the whistle, they would all be dead, and that it was in their interest to run away. With that warning all the enemy soldiers escaped and the people of Aiyetoro were left in peace. They gave thanks to Òrúnmìlà, and persuaded him to stay with them.

At divination, the person will be told that he is surrounded by enemies but that if he takes his own Ifá, he will overcome them. He should be advised that if he is proposing to travel, he should make sacrifice before going.

Chapter 11
Obara-Irete

```
I     I
I     I I
I I   I I
I     I I
```

He Made Divination for Plants to Become Trees:

Obara re-re-re Babalawo igi oko, odifa fun igi oko merin-din-lojo. That was the Awo who made divination for the 480 plants of the forest when they were coming to the world to become trees. They were told to make sacrifice. They all made sacrifice with the exception of Igi-eshin which refused to make sacrifice. That is why it could not grow to become a tree and remains the shortest of all plants.

When it appears at divination, the person will be advised to make sacrifice to avoid developing backache. The sacrifice is made with shea butter which the Ifá priest mixes with the Iyerosun of this Odù for the person to rub on his or her back.

The Divination He Made Before Leaving Heaven:

Uroke mi ege, uranke mi okun, idasi mi ogere. Adifa fun Òrúnmìlà baba ti kole orun bowa si kole aye.

My divination stick is held with care, my fly-whisk is as precious as beads, and my divination tray is golden, were the Awos who made divination for this Odù when he was coming from heaven. He was advised to serve: Ògún with a tortoise; his head with cock; Èsù with a small he-goat; and Ifá with a goat, to avoid having problems from women on earth. He made the sacrifice and came to the world.

He got married to a difficult woman who was having children who often died of convulsion. He invited Awos for divination in his house and he was advised to serve; Ifá with a goat, Èsù with a small he-goat for Èsù to eat alone, his head with a cock, and Ògún with a tortoise. He made the sacrifices and thereafter he did not lose anymore children. He began to prosper, but his modest success generated enmity.

Meanwhile, Egbere the wife of the Oloba of Oba began to show irresistible interest in him. Try as he did to discourage the woman, he could not stop her. He subsequently asked Ifá what to do and he was told to give a he-goat to Èsù. After the sacrifice he began a relationship with the woman and the Oloba not only surrendered her to him without let or hindrance, but later made him a high chief.

When this Odù appears at Ugbodu the person should make the sacrifice referred to above in order to survive the problems of women, child-deaths, and to prosper. At divination the person should be told that a woman is itching to marry him. He should marry the woman after giving a he-goat to Èsù.

He Made Divination for Onitiide:

Etutu nimu oko yeri egere gere. Ogigi lo fi enu iran sole.
Adifa fun Onitiide omo kango oju abeton ti kole orun si
kole aye. Alarini iku ko ngira

It is the ground that uses the hoe to shave his head. It is the sharp pointed digger that uses it's mouth to hit the ground with impunity.

These were the Awos who made divination for Onitiide when he was coming to live long on earth. He was told to make sacrifice with a sheep and a he-goat. When he got to the world, he had lots of problems. Enemies battered him from pillar to post, but he did not only outlive all of them, he also lived to a ripe old age.

The Contest for Supremacy Between Èsù and the Two Hundred Divinities:

When all the Two Hundred divinities got to they world, the decided to find out which of them was supreme. Òrìsà-Nlá, God's own surrogate, had meanwhile been accepted as the head of all the divinities on earth. However, Èsù told them that none of them was superior to him because "even God their father could not claim supremacy over him," (Èsù). At the first meeting of the earthly divine council, they all decided to be making a feast in turns beginning with Òrìsà-Nlá, and that whoever succeeded in making his feast without any let or hindrance, would be proclaimed as their generalissimo.

Once again, Èsù warned them that if he was not invited to start the feasting, no one would succeed in making one. He was hushed down as if he did not matter. With that decision Èsù withdrew from the conference.

Subsequently, Òrìsà-Nlá prepared the first feast and the table was laid for wining and dining. Just as the opening prayers were being said to the breaking of the kolanuts, Èsù went to the harem of Òrìsà-Nlá and blinked his eyes to two of his (Orisa-Nla's) children. The two children suddenly developed convulsion and there was a furor in the harem. The ensuing pandemonium attracted the divinities, but before help could reach the children, they both died. The feast could not materialize anymore.

Once again, Èsù appeared at the next meeting of the council to insist that he be allowed to begin the feasting. He was again told to disappear from the council chamber. It was the turn of Ògún to make his feast. He too lost two children without his elaborate feast materializing.

The same fate befell each of the other divinities, until it came to the turn of the divinity of wisdom. Òrúnmìlà consulted his Okeponrin and he was told to give a he-goat to Èsù adding the wooden images of a rabbit and a snake. He subsequently went ahead to prepare an elaborate feast. Èsù promised to surprise Òrúnmìlà pleasantly on account of the food and reverence he often gave to him.

As the kolanut was being split by Òrìsà-Nlá to begin the feast, Èsù turned the images of the snake and rabbit with which Òrúnmìlà made sacrifice, to live ones, and positioned them at the rubbish dump of Òrúnmìlà's house. The snake and the rabbit soon began to dance. The astonishment of the spectacle created a hubbub which disrupted the feast. As all the divinities come out to watch the strange event. The feast did not materialize, but on account of the sacrifice he made, Òrúnmìlà did not lose a soul.

At that stage, Èsù was invited to make his own feast, which he did successfully without any disturbance. Thereafter, all the divinities began to make their feasts successfully. That was how the eternal supremacy of Èsù was established, as a force to appease, and not to antagonize. When this Odù appears at divination, the person should be told to have his own Ifá and prepare his own Èsù to avoid incidence of child-death.

Divination for Sàngó When He Was Indisposed:

Obara-o-rote-nle, was a friend of Sàngó and he was trader. One day, before he returned from the market he was told that Sàngó had been taken ill and had been hospitalized away from home. He travelled to see Sàngó at the healing home to which he was taken with mental fatigue. When Obara-Irete got there he too became ill. The same physician that healed Sàngó also took care of him. He became well and had enough money to pay for his treatment but not enough to pay for Sango's treatment.

When he was returning home, Sàngó asked him to tell his relations to contribute money to pay for his treatment. One after the other, all of them however refused to help. All the brothers refused to help except the sister, the camwood (Osun-tree producing red powder) who decided to use herself to pay the physician in lieu of the cost of healing Sàngó. He however told her to take her brother home but that from then on, she should be sweeping and scrubbing for Sàngó, which she does to this day.

When Sàngó was returning home, he destroyed the homes of all his brothers, but has continued ever since to live with Osun, to this day.

When it appears at Ugbodu, the person should either prepare his own Sàngó or keep a thunder-stone in his Ifá shrine, to avoid sickness that would take him away from home. He should avoid having anything to do with a widow. He should expect to have lots of problems from his brothers. At divination the person should be advised; to be careful about women, and to serve Èsù with a he-goat.

Chapter 12
Obara-Eka

```
I I    I
 I    I I
I I   I I
I I   I I
```

His Harrowing Childhood:

When he was a child, he developed yaws which afflicted his entire body. His mother soon became fed up with the nuisance effect of the yaws. One day, she collected her two other children and abandoned Obara-Eka in the house. Since he was not in a position to help himself, he went about from one town and village to the other in search of his mother. Wherever he went he was told that a woman and two children had just left for the next town. He ended up at the backyard of an Oba's house where he got a hiding place inside a cave.

Everyday, he used to scan the rubbish dump at the back of the Oba's house for abandoned wastes to eat. One day, a palm wine tapper saw him from the top of the palm tree and alerted the Oba. The royal guards were subsequently told to watch out for him and he was presently apprehended. When he was brought before the Oba, he explained how he was abandoned by his mother and had to stay alive by picking food from incinerators and rubbish dumps. The Oba appointed one of his wives to take care of him and to be feeding him. He grew up to become an Ifá priest.

The Oba soon realized his importance and he was allowed to practice Ifism with the more elderly Ifá priests. He soon excelled in the practice and became a famous diviner. One day his mother was arraigned before the Oba, tried and found guilty of murder and sentenced to death by execution. Recognizing the mother, he could not resist the urge to identify himself. He sought and had an aside with the Oba, which gave him the opportunity of telling him, that the condemned woman was his mother.

The Oba reacted by asking her how many children she had and what became of them. She replied that she had three children out of which one died many years ago, while the other two had gone their separate ways. Obara-Eka was originally called Gbala, and it was during his exploits that he renamed himself Boripe. When asked whether she ever had a child called Boripe, she answered no. But the son explained to the Oba that he was originally called Gbala When the Oba asked her whether she ever had a son called Gbala she replied that he was the one that died. At that point, the son identified himself as the son who she abandoned to die because he had yaws. The woman became hysterical and began to weep.

The Oba subsequently changed the verdict to spare her life, and ordered that a goat and a hen should be slaughtered at the point where the woman was to have been executed. She was then released to return home with her son.

When this Ifá appears at Ugbodu, the person should be advised not to deride anyone. He is destined to leave the place of his birth to settle down elsewhere. He will be advised to serve Ifá with a goat which will be clubbed to death, before being used to serve Ifá, adding a hen, to avoid being penalized for an offense he knows nothing about. At divination, the person should serve Èsù with a he-goat to avoid an accusation of which he is innocent.

He Made Divination for Olofin to Avoid War:

Mo boju wo akpami otun, Ògún bara ka ija.
Mo boju wo akpami osi, Ògún bara ka etabi ago, etabi igbanyin.
Mo boju wo okankan, Ògún bara ka eta bi ogo, eta bi igbanyin.
Meeri aba mi, meeri'yemi. Mo ba mu uroke kpa Ògún.
Mo ba mu uroke kpa ogbon, moba mu da si Òrúnmìlà sin wonro ode odori koro koro.
Efun fun lele lari mo, aame r'Ògún oo.

I looked to the right and overheard the battle cries of war.
I also heard the mayhem of battle on my left, front and back
but I did not see the action and I did not see my parents.
If I had seen my parents besieged by the war,
I would have used my divination staff (Uranke) to kill twenty
persons, and would have used the fly-whisk (Oroke) to kill thirty
persons, and the divination tray to sack the rest of the town
of Odori. I only saw the wind of the war and not the war itself.

When it appears as Ure at divination, the person should be told he would hear the sound of war all around him, but that he should not worry because it would not affect him.

He Made Divination for the Setting Sun:

Ebara ka, Ebara ko, adifa fun ojo toon lo si okun-osa toon lo ra Ikara karaleru.

He made divination for the setting sun when he was going to the seaside to buy a slave. He was told to make sacrifice and he did and succeeded in buying the slave to bring home.

When it appears at divination for a man, he will be told that a woman is coming to marry him, but that he should make sacrifice with a hen. If the divinee is a woman, she will be told to make sacrifice with a cock in order to see a good husband to marry.

Made Divination for Olofin:

Ebara lili kii she hun ti akiki, Babaláwo to wa ni, be ni koo gbo fa. Odifa fun Olofin ate lu ma tu

Ebara the great, was not vast in the interpretation of Ifá divination. When it comes out at divination some Awos will order it to be closed because no one interprets it. But that will only happen because the Ifá priest does not understand what Òrúnmìlà is saying. That was the Awo who made divination for Olofin when he founded a new town that continued to flourish throughout his reign and outlived him. He was told to make sacrifice with a he-goat and he did.

Sacrifice Against Enmity:

Òrúnmìlà said that whoever has this Ifá at Ugbodu will have plenty of enemies among his blood relations. He recommended that the sacrifice should comprise three moulded sand (Esisu eru meta) three packets of salt, pieces of broken calabash, and three moulded mud (Oko epipu meta).

While he was preparing the sacrifice he chanted the following poem:

Pe e ni oguneru ma ntu.
Gere ni oguun iyo nse.
Oko akigaragba ki nrin eto.
Oniye bi ye ni oko epipu ma ntu.

The war of the dust breaks out suddenly.
The war of the salt happens softly.
The calabash does not break coherently.
The fragments of broken mud scatters.

When it appears at divination, the person will be told that enemies are at war with him, but that with sacrifice he will conquer them.

Divination Before He Left Heaven:

Before leaving heaven, he was told to make sacrifice because of the problems he was going to have from his relations. He was born of the same parents as the priests of Ògún, Olókun and Òsanyìn. He was advised to serve; Èsù with he-goat, and Ifá with a ram. He did the sacrifices before leaving heaven.

On getting to the world, he took to trading and the practice of Ifism. As soon as he began to register signs of modest success, his relations rose up in arms against him. Eventually, he went for divination and he was told to serve Èsù with cock and he-goat, and Ifá with a ram. After the sacrifices he got no more problems from his relations, and his prosperity began to blossom. Later, he took to Ifá practice and he was making itinerant divination visits to the reigning kings of the known world, which made him to become exceedingly wealthy and famous.

When this Ifá appears at Ugbodu, the person will be told to make sacrifice on account of the problems he is getting from his relations. At divination, he should be asked to make sacrifice with he-goat to Èsù.

He Made Divination for Alara-Isa, Omo Ajigbolu:

Alara-Isa was a very powerful king. Èsù however decided to create problems for him as a result of which his subjects stopped paying homage to him. Thereafter, Èsù advised the Alara to invite Obara-Eka to make divination for him. The Oba accordingly sent for the Ifá priest.

At the subsequent divination, he told the Alara-Isa that Èsù had crossed the road to his house with his legs and that anyone who struck his or her foot on Esu's legs was bound to die. That was why people became too scared to pay the traditional visits and homage to his palace. He advised the Oba to serve his divinities (Òsanyìn) with a ram and to make a feast with it, after giving a big he-goat to Èsù. He did the sacrifices after which Èsù removed his legs from the way and prosperity began to enter the palace once more. He compensated Obara-Eka with human and material gifts.

At divination, the person should be told that prosperity is eluding him. He should serve Èsù with a he-goat.

He Made Divination for the Owa of Ijesha:

After dealing with the Àlara, Èsù also proceeded to ferment difficulties for the Owa-Obokun of Ijesha by stopping prosperity from coming to him. The Owa invited Obara-Eka for divination after which he was advised to serve Èsù with a big he-goat and to make a feast with a ram after serving his Ifá with it. He did the sacrifice, and Èsù cleared the way for prosperity to resume visits to his palace. Obara-Eka was compensated with several human and material gifts.

Divinations for the Olowo of Owo, Ewi of Ado and the Ajero of Ijero:

Èsù created problems for these Oba because he wanted to help Obara-Eka, who became known as Obara Alayoka after he became a royal diviner and the diviner of the aristocracy. He was acclaimed and recognized by no less than sixteen kings of the known world. He became very wealthy and famous in the process.

Chapter 13
Obara-Eturukpon

```
I I     I
I I    I I
 I     I I
I I    I I
```

He Made Divinations for the Soldier-Ants, Earthworm and the Fly:

He made divination for the Soldier ants (Ijalo in Yorùbá and Okhian in Bini), Earthworm, (Ekolo in Yorùbá and ikolo in Bini) and the Fly (Eshinshin in Yorùbá and Ikian in Bini) warning them that war was imminent. Ijalo was told to serve Èsù with he-goat and a knife. Ekolo and Eshinshin were also told to serve Èsù with he-goat. Ijalo made the sacrifice but Ekolo did not. Rather than make sacrifice Eshinshin ran into the bush to build and hide in a house having no doors and windows. Meanwhile, war broke out.

Although Èsù directed the invading troops away from the direction of the soldier ants, he nonetheless used the knife with which they made sacrifice to equip their mouths as defense and attack weapons. As the soldier ants were running for cover, they ran into the invading forces. With the knives in their mouths, they attacked anyone who tried to assail them.

While the Earthworm was running for cover, he ran into the line of soldier-ants and they used their knives to cut him to pieces. While the war was still on, some people looted the palace of the Oba and went to hide the stolen properties in the house of Eshinshin. He was subsequently accused of stealing the Oba's properties and arranged for trial before the Oba. He had no defense and so was found guilty and sentenced to death by execution. Èsù however turned into a young girl to ask him whether he was not given to making divination. He confirmed that he did consult Òrúnmìlà but failed to make the recommended sacrifice. He begged the girl to go and make the sacrifice for him. The girl proceeded to make the sacrifice for him.

On the day of the execution, Èsù influenced the right hand man of the Oba and chief Judge to ask the Oba whether the fly was not too inconsequential to be killed. The Judge proposed that the fly should be warned not to live in the bush anymore, and that from then on, wherever two or more persons were gathered, he should dwell in their midst. That is why the fly has lived in the midst of people ever since.

When this Odù appears at Ugbodu, the person should be told that trouble is approaching. He should serve Èsù with a he-goat and a knife, in order to survive any strife.

At divination he should make the same sacrifice in order to avoid the risk of getting involved in a case or dispute he knows nothing about.

He Made Divination for the Elephant:

Ebara-Turukpon, odifa fun ori erin, abufun ijagbon re. He made divination for the head and the jaw of the elephant. They were advised to make sacrifice to avoid being abandoned in the forest after the rest of the elephant's body is taken home. Only the jaw made sacrifice. That is why after slaughtering the elephant in the forest, it is only the jaw that is taken home from the head. The rest of the head is abandoned in the forest.

When this Ifá appears at divination, the person will be told to make sacrifice so that his corpse might not get lost in the forest or very far away from home, after his death. He should make sacrifice with a small piece of white cloth and a he-goat.

He Made Divination for the Fay or Elf:

Ebara-turukpon, odifa Imere. He made divination for the Fay or Elf, (Igbakhuan in Bini) when he was coming to the world. He made the sacrifice with a he-goat and a fly-whisk (Oroke), but the father who was bringing him to the world did not make sacrifice to avoid losing the incoming child.

The child was born and on account of the sacrifice he made in heaven, he did not die at infancy. When he however grew to be an adult, he died suddenly. Before his death, he had become the economic mainstay of his parents. After his death, his parents became very poor. His father was a farmer. When he saw in heaven that his father was suffering on earth, he came with his friends to help in working at his father's farm.

When it was time for clearing the bush for a new farm, the father did a bit of brushing and went home. In the night, the son came with a team of fays to clear the entire stretch of forest for the father's farm. When it was time for felling trees, clearing stumps and digging ridges, the son came from heaven to help in a similar manner. The father decided to go for divination to find out who was the invisible hand that was assisting in his farm chores. He was advised to hide in the bush until midnight. He went to the farm to hide in the adjourning bush with a calabash plate in hand.

Just before midnight, he saw his dead son leading a team to the farm each carrying a fly-whisk. They dug all the ridges required for planting the yams and cocoyams. As they were working, the father went to remove his fly-whisk. They finished the work towards morning, Each of them collected their fly-whisks, but his son's was no where to be found. He searched in vain for it and when it was getting to sunrise, his friends left him to return to heaven. As soon as he found himself alone, he began to sing:

Oni mu urumi mumi,
Ebara tiele, Oloye, Ebara tiele.
Elegbe orun mei lo o,
Ebara tiele, oloye, Ebara tiele.

Following his failure to find his fly-whisk, he could not return to heaven without it. When it was sunrise, his father came out and held him. He queried the father for treating him the way he did, while his father queried him for leaving him for heaven the way he did. The father asked him whether he did not see how he had been suffering since he left and he replied, that was why he had been coming to lend a helping hand. The father insisted that it was not the same as living together. Convinced by the passionate appeal of his father, he had no option but to return home with him, since he lacked the power to return to heaven.

He however continued to search quietly for his fly-whisk, while his father made a point of keeping the key to his inner chamber, where he kept the fly-whisk outside the reach of anyone. After some time, the father relaxed his guard, thinking that his son had apparently decided to stay on earth for good. One day, his father drank excessively and became drunk. For the first time since his son returned, he removed the trouser containing the key to his inner chamber and hung it up in his living room. He subsequently fell fast asleep. When he found his father deeply asleep, he felt the pockets of the trouser and removed the key. He proceeded to open the inner room and searched until he found the calabash containing the fly-whisk. He opened it and removed the fly-whisk. Almost immediately, he set out for heaven where he reunited with his Elf colleagues in Hades.

When his father woke up, he discovered that his son had gone. After that experience it was no longer possible for the people of heaven to physically help anyone on earth.

When this Odù appears at divination, the person will be told to make sacrifice with a piece of white cloth, goat and calabash (Ugba or Okpan) so that his fay child might not leave him to return to heaven.

Made Divination for Sàngó:

Ki a fi igi lu igi; ki a ba le gbo ohun ti igi nwi.
Ki a fi okpe lu akpe ki a ba le gbo ohun ope.
Ki a fi obara eturukpon sode, ki a ri ibi gbo ohun enu omo Awo.
Omo Awo so sara, omo Awo so sako-sako-sara, ni edun nso igi.
Adifa fun Sàngó-Ogboja Olubebe mi omo arota were were segun.
Iwo Sàngó wa ru ebo ki iwo ma ba se inubi.

Hit two sticks against each other to hear their sound.
Hit two palmnuts against each other to hear the words of Òrúnmìlà.
Mark Obara-Eturukpon on the tray and listen to the revelations
of the Ifá priest.

These were the Awos who made divination for Sàngó. He was advised to make sacrifice with a ram and a piece of red cloth. He refused to make the sacrifice. When he was subsequently made a king, he arbitrarily killed a white dog, and buried a big goat alive. His subjects became annoyed and rebelled against him. He was subsequently dethroned and he went into the bush to commit suicide.

At that very moment, Ògún was returning from a war where he had been for several years. When Ògún saw Sàngó hanging from a rope, he cut the rope and Sàngó fell to the ground still breathing. He told Ògún and his followers not to let people know that he had hung himself. The people nonetheless began to ridicule him as the king who tried to hang himself. He reacted by executing those who were making jest of him. The people quickly changed their words to say that the king did not hang himself that is, "Oba Koso" in Yorùbá. That is how Sàngó earned the sobriquet of Oba Koso. The tree on which he hung himself is being referred to as "Igi a iyan." Eventually, he realized the high price he had paid for failing to make sacrifice, which explains why Sàngó remains short tempered to this day.

When the Odù appears at divination, the person will be advised to make sacrifice to avoid being short tempered.

He Made Divination for Olobara:

He made divination for Olobara, the priest of the water divinity, who danced from the bush to his house. He was told to make sacrifice to avoid the danger of leaving his tools in the bush. He reacted by deriding the Ifá priest and Èsù, while refusing to make the sacrifice. When Èsù was told that Olobara called him a thief and refused to make sacrifice, he (Èsù) turned himself into a creeping stem which positioned itself on the path of Olobara. As Olobara was returning home from the farm, the creeping stem stung his testicles and water gushed out. He abandoned all his instruments and raced home shouting for help, and crying that he had paid the price of refusing to make sacrifice.

When it appears at divination, the person will be advised to make sacrifice not to be involved in an accident before getting home from work.

He Made Divination for the Pumpkin and his Three Brothers:

He made divination for the Pumpkin advising him to make sacrifice on account of the problems he was going to have from his brothers on earth. He made the sacrifice with; a duck to his guardian angel, and a he-goat to Èsù.

The Pumpkin soon became a favorite to the people of the world. His three brothers Kola, Bitter Kola and Wild Kola, went to report him to God that he was disrupting the peace of the world. God told them to come with him to heaven. When he explained himself, God declared him innocent of all the charges and rubbed the white chalk of victory on his body. But he had failed to serve Èsù before leaving for heaven. On his way home Èsù caused a heavy rain to fall, which washed off the chalk of victory from his body.

When his brothers saw that the chalk had cleaned off, they claimed victory over him, before the people at home. On a second occasion, the brothers went again to God to report that he alone was fighting a whole community. After verifying the bad faith of his accusers, God again found him innocent and declared him victor. Once more, God rubbed his body with the white chalk of victory, which Èsù again cleaned off with a heavy downpour of rain. His brother once more claimed victory over him.

It was at that stage that he went for divination, and he was reminded of the he-goat he failed to give to Èsù. He quickly made the sacrifice and also served his head with a duck. Nonetheless, he was accused before God on a third occasion and once more, he was declared innocent. As God was rubbing the white chalk of victory on his body, he besought the Almighty Father to give him some of it to eat because even if his brothers caused the rain to wash off the chalk on his body, the rain could not clean the one inside his stomach. God then gave him some of the chalk to eat.

At that point God called his tree brothers and pronounced the following curses on them:-

"Kola   - you will always die on account of other people's problems."
"Bitter Kola - you will remain one bitter mass with no piece to split."
"Wild Kola   - you will have no use whatsoever for anyone."

On their way home, the rain again fell to wash off the chalk on the Pumpkin's body, but the one in his stomach appeared on his body after the rains stopped. On getting to the world he was applauded as the indisputable victor. That was the point at which people realized that he had been falsely accused all along.

When it appears at Ugbodu, the person should be warned to expect relentless problems from his relations. They will always bring his matter to the Cult of Witchcraft, but the king of the Night will invariably side with him provided he serves; the Night with a goat, Èsù with a he-goat, and his head with a duck. At divination he should serve Èsù with a he-goat and his head with a duck in order to be victorious over his enemies.

He Was Also Having Problems With Marriage:

Obara-Eturukpon had problems from his relations as well as from his marriage. He always seemed to marry the wrong women, who were never staying with him. When he went for divination, he was told to serve; Ifá with a goat, Èsù with he-goat, and his head with a duck. He was told that after performing the sacrifice he would marry the daughter of a king. He did the sacrifices.

Soon afterwards, he met a woman at a place where he was making divination for clients. The woman professed love to him and they subsequently got married. The woman turned out to be the daughter of the

Alara of Ilara. She stayed with him for keeps and gave birth to nine children.

At divination the person should make sacrifice in order to meet the right woman for marriage.

Chapter 14
Obara-Ose
Obara-Seke
Obara-Opere

```
    I      I
  I I    I I
    I    I I
  I I    I I
```

The Divination He Made Before Leaving Heaven:

Before leaving for the world, he was advised to make sacrifice because he was going to be very prosperous on earth, but would also have all the concomitant problems that go with it. He was told to make sacrifice at Orita-Ijaloko with a bundle of yam tubers, a head or bunch of plantains, corn and crushed yam, adding a bag of money. He performed the sacrifice, and went to God to receive blessing, before he left for the world.

On getting to earth, he took to farming and the practice of Ifism. He was not doing very well and could not afford the cost of marriage for a long time. He later invited other Awos to make divination for him on what to do to be able to make ends meet. At divination, he was told to make sacrifice with a bundle of yam tubers, corn, plantain bunch, and a bag of money.

He was told to decorate his Ifá shrine and to serve it with a hen and to serve his head with coconut. He was so poor that he had to borrow clothes to decorate his Ifá shrine. As he was slaughtering the hen for his Ifá, the blood soiled the borrowed cloth. He later returned the cloth to the woman from whom he borrowed it adding drinks and kolanuts.

One day he stood in front of his house very early in the morning, when he saw the daughter of the Oba called Seke passing by. She greeted him, and after the exchange of greetings, the girl told him that she came to visit him. He took her inside the house and she told him that she was offering herself in marriage to him because she had for long, observed that he had no wife. He replied that he was only a poor farmer and could not afford to maintain a wife. She insisted all the same in marrying him.

After living with him for four days, she decided to return home to report her decision to her father. On getting home she told the father that she had seen the man she wanted to marry. The father reacted by asking her to invite the man to come and see him. When she got back to Òrúnmìlà's house she told him that her father wanted to see him. He was afraid to go because he did not have a presentable attire to wear. She insisted that he was not being invited to parade his wealth and that he had no cause to be afraid. Following that reassurance, he decided to go with her.

When they got to the palace, the Oba found Obara-Ose to be a very handsome man. He immediately agreed to the marriage and invited his treasury keeper to collect treasures for the daughter to take to the husband's house. The Oba told him that he did not want any dowry but should be paying homage to him annually. After blessing the marriage, he prayed for the couple and they left.

Meanwhile, his wife began trading with the capital given to her by the father. His own farming also began to flourish. He was soon able to build his own house. At the end of the year, he loaded the best yams from his harvest and sent them to his father-in-law, adding plantains, corn, and kolanuts. He made the wife to sell plenty of the yam harvest in the market. Meanwhile at the market Olokun's daughter found the yams very attractive and when she was told that they were from Òrúnmìlà's farm, she offered to meet him.

When the market dispersed, Olokun's daughter took her bag and went with Akpetebi to meet Òrúnmìlà. They did not know that the visitor was the daughter of Olókun. Before leaving the market for Òrúnmìlà's house, she dispatched the pages who followed her to the market after telling them that she was returning home in five days time.

After exchanging pleasantries with Òrúnmìlà, Olokun's daughter told him that she came to marry him. He replied that he had nothing, being a simple farmer. She however reassured him that his farming was enough. Five days later, she left for home, promising to return with her belongings.

It was after she returned with her luggage of wealth that they realized she was the daughter of Olókun himself. She subsequently told Seke, the senior wife, to stop going to the market. She added that her followers would thenceforth be trading for the family. Òrúnmìlà subsequently became very prosperous. When the Oba saw how prosperous Obara-Ose had become, he made him the Shasere and Prime Minister of the kingdom.

He Made Divination for the Two Men Who Learned How to Make Tribal Marks:

Momo momo, ko je ki Awosi kola bi ukpere. Odifa fun akpere, abunfun Awosi.

The all-knowing syndrome prevented Awosi from attaining the same level of proficiency as Ukpere, was the name of the Awo who made divination for Akpere and Awosi when they were going to heaven to learn how to make tribal marks. When they got to the bodymaker of heaven, Akpere was the first to learn how to do the markings. After completing the markings on Akpere, it was the turn of Awosi. As soon as one marking was inscribed on the back of Awosi he told the teacher that he already knew how to do it all. The teacher then dispatched them to return to earth to be doing the markings to others the way he did it on them.

Akpere was able to design tribal marks in various ways, but on getting home Awosi only knew how to make the single marking. He did not know how to do the others. That is why some tribes only have one tribal mark, while others have several.

When this Odù appears at divination, the person will be advised to be patient and humble in the business or trade he is learning in order to know all there is to know about the profession. He should avoid a know-all stance.

He Made Divination for Okpere, the Slave of Onidoko:

Obara-ose kii she fun elomii, enida obara ose, oun ni ebara ose she fun. Adifa fun okpere eyi tiin she eru Onidoko atijo. Onidoko fu omi oju she bere omo. Okpere she Awo fun.

Obara-ose does not manifest for others except those for whom he appears at divination and who make the prescribed sacrifice. That was the Awo who made divination for Okpere, the slave of Onidoko, when he was going to use Awo art to solve the problems of Onidoko.

When Okpere found his master lamenting for having no children, he decided to help him. He prepared the necessary medicine for his master and his wives to use. Thereafter, he travelled out for Awo practice. By the time he returned from the tour, Onidoko's wives had each given birth to a child and there was visible happiness in the family. Onidoko then thanked Okpere for helping him, and he showed his appreciation by granting him (Okpere) freedom from servitude.

When this Odù appears at divination, the person should be advised to take his servants and those working for him into confidence. They might help in solving his problems.

He Made Divination for Onidoko:

Orisa le she odifa fun Okpere tiinshe eru Onidolo atijo.

After Onidoko became an Oba, Okpere was still going to make divination for him. Before he had the opportunity of doing so, Onidoko was removed from the throne, because his people and his household turned against him. Onidoko then sent for Okpere to come and help him. After making divination, Okpere told Onidoko to make sacrifice with he-goat, cock and Guinea-fowl. He assured Onidoko that after the sacrifice his people would come looking for him.

After eating his he-goat, Èsù proceeded to cause general deprivation and suffering in the town. When the situation became unbearable, they went for divination where they were told that there would be no peace and prosperity in the town unless they persuaded Onidoko to return to the throne. The people immediately sent elders to go and beg Onidoko for armistice and to return to the throne. He later thanked Okpere by making him a chief.

When it appears at divination the person will be advised to make sacrifice so that whatever problems he has at home and in his place of work, might abate.

Divination for Him When He Was Going on Tour:

When he was going on tour for Ifá practice he was told to make sacrifice so that he might succeed in returning home with whatever gifts he got during the tour. He was told to serve his head with four pigeons, but he only served his head with two pigeons. He went to work in a town where there were relatively stronger Awos.

On getting to the town, he was told that he was invited to help them in performing the annual festivals of three divinities in the town. They tied up a ram, a goat and a dog and he was asked to disclose which animal was going to be used for serving which divinity.

To complicate the puzzle, they had arranged the animals as follows:-

The divinity eating ram had a dog tied to its shrine,
The divinity eating dog had a ram tied to its shrine, and
The divinity eating goat had the goat tied to its shrine.

He however succeeded in unraveling the puzzle, by giving ram to the divinity eating ram, dog to the divinity eating dog and slaughtered the goat tied to the goat-eating divinity.

Instead of applauding his proficiency, they prepared an even more fatal test for him. He was sent to the eldest woman of the town who was to keep him talking while they finalized arrangements for killing him. When he got to the old woman's place, he told her that she was ill with eye trouble and she confirmed it. He then told her that he had seen a leaf at the back of her house which he would prepare for her to use in treating the eyes. On that pretext, he left the old woman purportedly to fetch the leaves.

As soon as he entered the bush, he ran away from the place and found his way home, without eating out of the meat he had slaughtered to the three divinities. That is why it is often said that Obara-Ose was the Babaláwo who slaughtered meat for divinities without eating out of it. If he had used all four pigeons to serve his head, he might have avoided the tests.

When this Ifá appears at Ugbodu, the person will travel out soon afterwards. Before travelling however, he should serve his Ifá with a ram so that he might return home with the gifts he would receive from the tour. At divination, the person should serve Èsù with a he-goat.

He Made Divination for the Mother of Ògún:

Ire la kola, a komo ala'be.
Ipere e d'osu, a mo aworo ti o da loshu.
Atele'wo ni a ba ila, a a m'eni ti o ko-o.
Firi ni a ri oji-ji, a o mo irin ti o rin ti o fi nte
le enia-l'ehin.

We see the tribal marks on the body, without knowing the marker.
A young mortal became a divinity, but no one knew the priest who
prepared him as a divinity.
We see the marks on the palm but know not who marked to.
We see the shadow but not the feet with which it walks behind one.

Those were the four Awos who made divination for Lagboburu, the mother of Ògún. Lagboburu was barren when she left for the hilltop where she saw a hen with it's chicks. She began to weep over her own difficulties, after exclaiming that it was after all the same God that could not wipe her tears with childbirth that gave all those children to the hen.

From nowhere she heard a voice commanding her to stop crying and to go for divination and sacrifice, because she was destined to have great children. She came down immediately from the top of the hill and went to Òrúnmìlà for divination. At divination, she was advised to make sacrifice with ten rabbits, a hen that hatched 10 chickens, ten bats, palm nuts, and plenty of drinks. She made the sacrifice.

Not long afterwards, she became pregnant and gave birth to a male child who brought a miniature hammer and spear from the womb. She eventually gave birth to four other children. Right from infancy her first son was always very pugnacious. He was always troubleshooting all over the place. When the trouble he was causing became embarrassing, his mother took him to Òrúnmìlà for divina-tion. It was then she was told that her son was the great Ògún himself. Thereafter, Òrúnmìlà used the following incantation to humour the child:

Inu ni o ti nre efo ebo lowa.
Inu no o ti nre ewe koko wa.
Ati owo ati ese, oku ki la 'gbara.
Oni bi orun bi orun ni o nshe eye ope.

Almost instantaneoulsy, the child fell to the ground and began sprawling and begging Òrúnmìlà to give him food to eat. Òrúnmìlà said that he should be chained before being given any food. He was accordingly chained to the floor after which Òrúnmìlà slaughtered a dog and gave him its blood to drink, followed by the palm wine and palm oil. Those were the first sacrifices made to Ògún.

When this Odù appears at divination, the person will be told that he has a barren woman in his family who is crying desperately to have children. She should be advised to make sacrifice to have a child. She is destined to give birth to a powerful child.

Chapter 15
Obara-Ofun
Obara-Mo-Ofun

```
I I    I
I      I I
I I    I I
I      I I
```

Made Divination for the Parrot When He Tried to Learn Ifá:

Mo ti mo Obara, mo mo ofun, Babaláwo odidere odifa fun odidere
n'ojo ti yi o lo ko Ifá lowo Awoko.

He made divination for the parrot when he was going to learn Ifism from a priest called Awoko. He was advised to make sacrifice. He did not however see the need for it when he only wanted to study the art. Without making the sacrifice, he left for the house of Awoko to begin the course. As soon as Awoko pronounced the name of Obara-Ofun, Èsù overwhelmed the parrot with a know-all syndrome and he told his teacher that he had known all he was required to learn. Awoko, who felt needlessly interrupted, asked him whether it was not Ifá he wanted to learn. The parrot replied as if possessed "moti mobara, mo mofun," which has remained the call sign of the parrot to this day. Thus, Obara-and-Ofun remained the only two words the parrot knew in the Ifá literary corpus, because of the sacrifice he refused to make.

When this Odù appears at divination, the person will have the habit of being a fast talker. He should however be told to be careful not to allow the words of his mouth to commit him negatively. He should also be told not to behave as if he knows more than his boss or teacher. Generally, he should avoid a tendency to an all knowing disposition, to avoid losing the benefits of humility and modesty.

When this Odù appears on the floor or it is written on the tray, nobody should eat any food in the room. Whoever wants to eat should move elsewhere to eat the food.

Divination for Him Before Leaving Heaven:

When he was coming to the world, he went for divination and he was told to make sacrifice on account of the problems he was going to encounter from his household and from women. He was told to make sacrifice with; a he-goat to Èsù, and to make a feast with a goat. He was advised to have nothing to do with light-complexioned women. He was also advised never to drink any alcohol to obviate the danger of lunacy. He made all the sacrifices. Nonetheless, a yellow woman followed him to the earth all the way from heaven.

He got to the world to become a proficient Ifá priest. He came out of Ife, but was practicing Ifism up to Oyo. It was at the pinnacle of his career that he met the yellow woman who followed him from heaven. On one occasion he was invited by the Aláàfin of Òyó to come and make divination for him. That was where he met the yellow woman and they were attracted to each other as if they had known themselves all their lives.

He did successful work for Alaafin for which he was aptly compensated. At the head of the list of gifts given to him was a man and the light skinned woman with whom he had fallen in love. He returned home to Ife with the woman. When his relations saw the gifts he brought from Oyo, they became envious and began to ferment trouble for him. His fortunes soon began to flag. At the same time, since the yellow woman followed him from heaven to destroy him, she began her morbid contrivances by poisoning food for him to eat. He immediately developed a severe cough.

The cough soon began to disrupt his physical zeal to work. When it degenerated to the point at which he began to vomit blood, he went to the more elderly Awos of Ifá for divination. When they sounded Ifá for him, his own Odù appeared. He was told that his problem sourced from his own household. He was also reminded of his heavenly injunction (which he could not remember) not to have anything to do with a yellow wife. The Awos however prepared the requisite medicine with palm wine and a big bat (Oloja owonron or Owo) to cure his cough, while advising him to make a feast with a goat for his household after giving he-goat to Èsù. They assured him that the danger of death had abated although he would continue to cough lightly.

He made the feast accordingly, after which those troubling him began to leave his house at the instigation of Èsù. All his relations who were living with him and who were responsible for the deterioration in his business, left entirely. His yellow wife did not leave but she became disillussioned, frustrated and incapacitated. He however began to prosper once more and the yellow wife later returned to heaven.

When this Ifá appears at Ugbodu, the person should be advised; not to allow any relation to live or stay with him, not to have anything to do with a yellow woman, not to drink alcohol, and to feast his household with a goat after serving Èsù with he-goat and a big bat.

He Made Divination for Ataparapa, the Armed Bandit:

Ataparapa was a ruthless bandit who was so vast in diabolical charms that no one was able to assail him. After he became convinced that no one on earth was going to be able to harm him, he went to Obaramo-Ofun for divination on what to do to insure himself against Death. He was told to make sacrifice with a he-goat, a small pot containing a sponge and the blood of the he-goat. After making the sacrifice, he decided to travel to heaven to befriend the divinity of Death.

In the course of his interaction with Death, he was able to know that the materials with which he made sacrifice on earth were the very things that Death forbade - viz, small clay pot, sponge and blood. With that knowledge he returned to earth and continued his banditry with impunity. He became an even more rapacious menace to his community and no one knew what to do with him.

In those days, Death usually came to the world to remove people who were adjudged to be thorns in the flesh of their neighbours or communities. When an appeal was made to Death to remove Ataparapa to heaven, he decided to pay him a visit. When Death got to the house of his friend, he met him sitting with a small clay pot, and a sponge with blood spilled all over the place. At the sight of his taboos,

Death quickly ran back to heaven.

When the people in the community saw that Death could not remove him, they persuaded his wife to tell them what he forbade. She decided to co-operate with them because she too was disgusted with the embarrassment his actions had brought to the family. She told them that the only thing he forbade was ripe plaintain, and that he would die the very day he ate it.

The people immediately arranged to use ripe plaintain to prepare wine (Oten) for him do drink, since he was always eating about. After drinking the plaintain wine, he returned home to ask his wife to shave the small Osu hair at the center of his head, where his strength lay. He subsequently fell asleep and never woke up. His death however created many other unpleasant ripples for the family.

At Ugbodu and at divination, the person should beware of women generally. He should give; a goat to Ifá, a dog to Ògún, and a he-goat to Èsù so that a woman might not betray him to his enemies. He should forbid plaintain wine.

Made Divination for Òrìsà-Nlá when Coming to the World:

Ebara fifun kpeneden - odifa fun Òrìsà-Nlá Oshereigbo ounti
kole orun bo wa si kole aye.

He made divination for God's own surrogate on earth Òrìsà-Nlá, when he was coming to the world. He was told to make sacrifice in order to command universal and eternal honor and respect. He made the sacrifice with a ram and white cloth. On getting to the world, he became the overseer of all of God's creatures on earth and he was revered by all.

He Divined for his Wife to Have a Child:

Shu waju kimi si en, Arisini ko suan. Eni ti a sin iwaju
l'ongbe. Adifa fun alabake t'in she aya Ebara mo ofun t'on
tun to ri to'mo difa.

Lead the way and let me follow. Whoever is being led stays in front, were the two Awos who made divination for Alabaake, the wife of Obara-Ofun when she was eager to have a child. She was told to make sacrifice with two hens and a pigeon. She did the sacrifice and began to have children.

Made Divination for Majawote, the Mother of the Sun:

Eye kekere of'oju wo ogbe, oshudi kpiri kpiri. Adifa fun maa ja'wote t'inshe yeye ojo.

A small bird flew into the bush, and the anus became enlarged, were the names of the Awos who made divination for Maajawote, the mother of daylight or sun. She was told to make sacrifice with a cock, white cloth and a broom. She made the sacrifice and gave birth to daylight which everybody reveres and look forward to meeting, but which no one looks on the face.

Made Divination for Igbayinrin When She Divorced Her Husband:

Se se se, wo wo wo. Adafa fun Igbayinrin aya Egboro, onfi
Egboro si le, olo fe Olugbo.

Those were the two Awos who made divination for Igbayinrin, the wife of Egboro when she was going to leave her husband to marry Olugbo. They advised her not to leave her husband because he was her man from heaven and that it would amount to straying away from the path of her destiny if she did. She was too intoxicated with the new wine of Olugbo to listen to the advice of Ifá. She went ahead and moved to live with Olugbo.

When she began to suffer in Olugbo's house she returned to the two Awos for divination and they reminded her of the warning they gave her before she left Egboro. They told her that she would not have a settled life anymore unless she returned to Egboro. She subsequently went to apologize to Egboro who agreed to have her back. When she moved back to her husband, her relations began to make jest of her by saying:-

Igbayinrin aya Egboro,
Oto ki ewa rele,
Oko aro.
Igbayinrin the wife of Egboro

It is time for you to return home
To your destined husband.

When this Odù appears at divination for a woman, she will be advised not to contemplate leaving her husband because she will regret the action.

He made divination for the Oba of Benin:

Bi Oba mo Ifá olida, eni oni fuen nifa mi da.
Bo ba mo ibo gede, emi oni fuen ni ibo mi gba
Adifa fun Oba Ado nijo to fi omi o ju shubere omo.

If you know Ifá, I will not give you my own Ifá to sound for me. If you know how to cast Ibo divination, I will not give you mine to cast for me. Those were the Awos who made divination for the Oba of Benin when he was anxious to have children. He was told to make sacrifice with a goat and two hens. He made the sacrifice after which most of the women in his harem began to have children.

The Poem of Obara-mo-Ofun:

In a dialogue with his Ifá priest, Òrúnmìlà said:-

Olobara fun ti lo ti lo
Olobara fun ti jon ti jon
Enikan kole so fun pe ki omo eku ko ma dele eku.
Enikan ko le so fun pe ki omo eja ko ma dele eja.
Enikan ko le so fun pe ki omo eye ko ma dele eye.
Enikan ko le so fun pe ki omo eran ko ma dele eran.
Enikan ko le so fun pe ki omo eni ko ma wole eni.

Olobara should press on from all sides, because;
No one can stop the rat from visiting the rat,
No one can stop the fish from visiting the fish,
No one can stop the bird from visiting the bird,
No one can stop the animal from visiting the animal, as
No one can stop the human being from visiting a human being.

Òrúnmìlà advised that for mankind to interact beneficially, sacrifice should be made with; chalk, camwood and honey.

The eyes of the white chalk forbid seeing the dangers in Benin:
Just as the eyes of red camwood forbid, seeing
the dangers of Ekiti.

And the eyes of the bee forbid, seeing the danger in the hole of a tree.

When this Odù appears at divination, the person will be advised to make sacrifice to avoid a repeat performance of the wickedness of which he had once been a victim. Òrúnmìlà promises to prevent him from becoming the victim of wickedness once more.

IFISM
The Complete Works of Òrúnmìlà

Volume Seven
The Odus of Okonron

I I
I I
I I
  I

Chapter One
Okonron-Ogbe
Okonron-Mi-Sode
Okonron-Ohun-Olode

```
I    I I
I    I I
I    I I
I      I
```

He Made Divination for the Two Hundred divinities When They Tried to Bring Prosperity to the World:

After the creation of the earth by God, the divinities discovered that it was bare and that they required the good things of life to make the world livable. They all trooped to heaven to ask God to give them the instruments of a happy life on earth. Before leaving for heaven they all went for divination to the following diviners:

Egena ofo mi serun ku.
Ogbologbo ure logbe inu ogan.
Ofi ohun okunrin yoro yoro.
Adafa fun awon igba erumole won fe lo gba ure wa ye lodo Olodumare.

The live fire wood drank water through its mouth and quenched.
It is a strong porcupine that bellows like a man from within
the ant hill.

These were the Awos who made divination for the Two Hundred divinities when they were going to God to collect the instruments of prosperity for living on earth. In response to their request, God opened the treasure house of heaven for them to collect whatever they wanted. Before going to the treasury, they were advised at divination to make sacrifice with corn cake (Elekute or Adidan in Yorùbá and Uloka in Bini), sugar cane, bean pudding (moyin moyin) and Oroke (fly whisk). When they left the diviner's place, they went into conference among themselves and wondered what force deserved to receive sacrifice from them after God had willingly made the gifts available to them. They resolved that the sacrifice was super- fluous, not withstanding the fact that the materials for it were tenuous and commonplace.

Òrúnmìlà however told them that he was going to make the sacrifice because God had much earlier demonstrated that disruptive forces could deprive them of their fortune if they did not appease them. After jeering at Òrúnmìlà as the father of sacrifice, they insisted that they were not going to make any sacrifice.

Òrúnmìlà nonetheless collected the materials and went to make the sacrifice. He also added a he-goat for Èsù, knowing that he required his support. The Awos made the sacrifice after which they gave him the elekute, sugar can, honey and moyin-moyin to keep in his bag for the journey. He was advised to give them to Elenini, who was bound to accost him on his return journey. After slaughtering the he-goat for Èsù, they used the skin to prepare a small drum which he was given to travel with in his bag.

After telling God what they wanted, He cleared them to remove whatever they could carry from the treasury to base. In consonance with the advice he was given by the diviners, Òrúnmìlà was the last get to the heavenly treasury. Elenini the treasury keeper, had meanwhile transfigured into a ferocious cripple to confront each of the divinities on their return journey to earth.

One after the other, he seized all the materials they collected from the treasury and returned them to base. In consonance with the advice he was given by the diviners, Òrúnmìlà was the last to embark on the return journey to earth.

When he finally met the cripple, he was stopped on his track and he told the fearsome creature that he had gifts for him. He first gave him honey, followed by sugar cane, elekute and moyin moyin. As the cripple was eating, Èsù emerged to advise Òrúnmìlà to start beating his drum to the following song accompaniment: Aro oludena gburu, ki ejo aro oludena. Meaning that he was going to the world with the good things required for a happy life.

As he was singing and drumming, the cripple took the fly-whisk (Oroke) from Òrúnmìlà and began to dance. When Èsù saw the cripple dancing, he took the drum from Òrúnmìlà. As soon as Èsù took over the beating of the drum, the cripple turned towards the direction of heaven while Òrúnmìlà continued his journey towards the earth. That was how Òrúnmìlà ended up as the only divinity that succeeded in reaching the earth with the instruments of prosperity he collected from heaven.

When this Ifá appears at Ugbodu, the person will be told that unless he makes sacrifice, obstacles will not allow his destiny and the wishes he made in heaven, to actualize on earth. At divination the person, if a man, should be told to have his own Ifá, and if a woman, she should be told to marry an Ifá man or persuade her husband to have his own Ifá, they are to prosper.

The Divination He Made Before Leaving Heaven:

Eni to n gbofa ko i ru'ude. Eni to r'ude ko gbofa. These were the two Awos who made divination for Okonron-ro-Ode when he was leaving heaven. He was advised to make sacrifice with a he-goat to Èsù. He made the sacrifice and became an Ifá priest on getting to the world. He had been warned at divination to beware of flirtation on earth.

He had two friends on earth; Sasagele-Ule and Sasagele-Oko. On one occasion he travelled to a place called Egbe for Ifá practice. A woman who came to him for divination professed love to him. Without knowing that the woman was married he requited her love. After making love to her, some informants told the husband, who reacted by arranging for his assassination. When his friend Sasagele-Ule heard of the plot to kill him, he went to Sasagele-Oko to carry a message to Okonron-so'de, that he was required to return home at once because his father was at the point of death.

Sasagele-Oko went at once to carry the message to Okonron-so-ode, who immediately packed his bag and headed for home. His two friends however planned to rendezvous with him at the last road junction to Egbe, where they told him that there was nothing wrong with his father, but that they used the story to lure him to leave the town because there was a plot to assassinate him that night for seducing somebody's wife. He left for home immediately.

When this Ifá appears at Ugbodu, the person will be told to beware of flirtation. A friend will however save him from the trouble his is bound to have on account of a woman. A widow would offer herself to him in marriage, but he should refuse to marry her.

At divination, he should be told to serve Èsù with a he-goat to avoid trouble emanating from a woman.

How He Solved the Problem of Having Children:

Odide ogbo omu ori ke fun. Agbo gbo'gbe jojore guale. Eje omode ra ga ga ga.

These were the three Awos who made divination for Okonron-so-ode when he did not have children early enough in life. He was told to serve; Ifá with a hen, and Èsù with a he-goat. He made the sacrifice and the Ifá priests prepared medicines for him to give to his wife. Not long afterwards, his wife became pregnant. They also told him to advise the wife to be sweeping and scrubbing the house regularly, because Ifá was annoyed with her. She gave birth to the child and had several other children subsequently.

Made Divination for Elekole When His Dog Was Missing:

Akasho leri, Awo ode Ewi ado, asho Ibante, Awo ode Offa. Okan gologolo Awo elekole. Adifa fun Elekole ni jo ti efuuru aja re tu sonu to a wo kiri.

These were the three Awos who made divination for the Elekole of Ikole-Ekiti when his favorite dog was missing. After divination, the first two Awos from Ado Ekiti and Offa told the Elekole to forget about the dog because it was either already dead or trapped.

The third Awo however told him to make sacrifice with a cock, fish, rat, eko and akara and that before long, the dog would return home. The sacrifice was quickly made. When the person who carried the sacrifice to Èsù was returning to the house, he saw the dog running home. Elekole rejoiced and thanked Okan gologolo.

Made Divination for Eda Lausa When He Was Very Poor:

Agbe lofi ibi woroko showa.
Aluko lofi ibi woroko sho'sun.
Eje omode titun misa gara misa goro ninu Awo.
Won difa fun eda Laausa nijo to maa sho on udu tiko gbofa.

The bird called Agbe converted misfortune to money.
The bird called Aluko generated fortune by turning
a deformed tree to a camwood producer.
The blood of an infant does no congeal in a pot.

These were the three Awos who made divination for Eda-Lausa when he was poor. He was told to have his own Ifá in order to get out of his poverty. The three Awos accordingly prepared Ifá for him. They also prepared an Ifá bracelet (Ude) for him to wear on his wrist. To make a new start in life, he was advised to leave the land of his birth to settle down in a new town, but to wear his bracelet regularly night and day. He accordingly left home to live in a new town, where, for a living, he resorted to fetching fire wood to sell.

In the new town, Olofin's favorite wife was barren. Several divine priests had prepared medicines for her to have a child to no avail. When she saw her menstruation that month, she informed the Oba, who told her to soak her menstrual pad inside a pot and bring it to him.

The Olofin himself made Ifá divination on whether the blood on that pad was going to produce a child. Okonron-mi-sode appeared at divination. He subsequently invited all his Ifá priests to interpret the divination. One after the other, all of them tried but missed the point. Next, the Olofin sent invitations across to the following Babalawos:

Mo le ki Ògún, Awo Alara,
O-ki-ki-ki, ko le tu n mo,
Mo le i ogbon, Awo Ajero,
O-ki-ki-ki, ko le fun bo,
Mo li ki, Awo Opatoromofin,

They were the famous Ifá priests to the Alara, Ajero and to aristocracy. They all came but could not translate the Ifá on the tray. He then asked whether there was any other Awo in the Ife kingdom remaining to be invited. He was told that there was one who used to sell firewood with an Ifá bracelet on hand but no one seemed to know where he lived. He immediately issued a search-and-find order for him.

When the searchers eventually caught up with him, he was just returning from the forest with a load of fire wood. When Olofin's message was delivered to him, he decided to accompany the messengers at once to the palace. Upon arrival, Olofin showed him the Ifá on the tray and asked him whether he could interpret it. When he replied that the Ifá on the tray was his own Odù but that he did not know how to interpret Ifá, he was told to explain why he was wearing the Ifá bracelet (Ude) on his wrist. He began to mention the names of the Ifá priests who prepared the Ude for him. By the time he mentioned the name of the third Awo (Eje omo titun misa gara misa goro nunu Awo) Olofin exclaimed that he had solved the riddle, and that if others had mentioned that much, the need to look for him would not have arisen. He was asked whether he knew the relevant sacrifice going with it. Èsù instantly took over his mind and as if possessed, he declared that it required ten rats, ten fishes, ten cocks, ten hens, ten goats, ten men, ten women, ten rams, ten akara, ten eko and ten bags of money.

The materials were produced and he made the sacrifice, Olofin went inside and brought out his ASE to pronounce the curse of death on anyone who would try to undo this innocent Awo. The following month, the favorite wife of Olofin became pregnant and in the fullness of time, gave birth to a male child. That also marked the beginning of prosperity for Eda-Lausa. He gave up selling fire wood and subsequently became a proficient Ifá priest.

When this Odù appears for a man or a woman anxious to have a child, he or she should be advised to ask Ifá priests to prepare Ude for him or her. If he already has Ifá, he should learn Ifá art. If not, he should have his own Ifá. For a woman, she should be advised to marry an Ifá man. The person is a fay (Imere or Igbakjuan) but Òrúnmìlà will be able to change his or her fortune to live on earth.

Made Divination for Ololo, the King of Fays or Elfs:

Fiiri Jakande, Jakande Fiiri. Adifa fun Ololo tiin she Olori egbe.

Those were the two Awos who made divination for the king of Fays (Imere in Yorùbá and Igbakhuan in Bini). They told him that he had overstayed his life span on earth because his followers in heaven were waiting for him. Since he was enjoying life on earth, so much that he had no wish to return to heaven, his followers had embarked on a policy of damaging his belongings and activities on earth. He went for divination to know why his things were spoiling. He was advised to make sacrifice with rat, fish, hen, pigeon, snail, akara and eko, and to feast his fay followers by making Sarah with a goat. He was also advised to have his own Ifá after making the feast. He complied fully with the advice and it was only then that his followers abandoned him to Òrúnmìlà to live on earth.

When the Odù appears at divination for a woman, she will be advised to marry an Ifá man or to encourage her husband to have his own Ifá if she is to live long on earth. If the divinee is a man, he will be advised to take his own Ifá. To be on the safer side, he should make a feast for his followers.

Òrúnmìlà Declares Ude As An All-Purpose Protector:

Òrúnmìlà ni ki a ji sode.
Moni ki Olokonron sode.
Oni ti omo eku ba ti ji, oni o sode babare m'owo
Oni ki a ji sode, Moni ki Olokonron sode.
Oni ki omo eja ba ji, ki o sode baba re m'owo.
Oni ki omo eye ba ji, oni ki a sode baba re m'owo.
Oni ki aji sode, Moni ki Olokonron sode,
Oni ki a so fun omo eni, ba ti ji, ko o sode
babare m'owo.

Òrúnmìlà recommends that we should,
wake up and wear our amulet.
Because the children of the rats, fishes, birds, and
animals, wake up in the morning to wear the protective
amulets prepared by their parents.
Human beings should also wear their protective
amulets prepared by their parents.
Human beings should therefore wear their protective
bracelets (Ude) on their wrist when they wake up in
the morning to protect them against the danger of
untimely death.
Asked what is to be used to prepare the amulet,
he enumerated them as; rats, fishes, a hen about
to lay eggs and the special Ifá beads worn by chiefs.

He concluded that any person who develops the habit of wearing it soon after waking up in the morning will never be the victim of sudden death.

When this Odù appears at divination, the person will be told that a child is on the way to him or her, but that the baby should be made to wear Ifá beads on its wrist when born, so that it may not die.

This is how this Odù earned the sobriquet ot Okonron-Ohun-Olode.

Chapter Two
Okonron-Oyeku
Okonron-Aronmo

```
I I    I I
I I    I I
I I    I I
I I     I
```

Divination Before Leaving Heaven:

Uroke mi lawo ligonrin, Oroke mi lawo le'turuye were the two Awos who made divination for this Odù when he was leaving heaven. He was advised to make sacrifice because he was going to have several enemies on earth. He was told to serve Èsù with a he-goat and roasted yam and he did the sacrifice.

As soon as he got to the world, a mark was put on his forehead by the Cult of Witchcraft to enable witches to identify him wherever he went, as a victim marked out for destruction.

One night, while he was sleeping, he had a dream in which his guardian angel told him to wash his head with a he-goat on Èsù shrine. When he got up in the morning, he made divination and Ifá told him that the sacrifice was to enable Èsù to remove the mark inserted on his forehead by Awon Iyami Osoronga. Before then, he had been experiencing all kinds of difficulties. Everything he touched always went wrong. He however proceeded to make the sacrifice after which the witches began to confess to what they had been doing against him.

Before then, he had developed a chronic stomach ache which refused to yield to any form of treatment. One morning, a woman having one eye came to give him leaves and materials to cook and eat to cure his stomach trouble. After eating the preparation, he vomited a scorpion which ended his stomach trouble.

When this Odù appears at divination, the person should be told to get Ifá priests to wash his head on Èsù shrine with a he-goat to minimize his problems from witchcraft. He also probably has a stomach problem which was caused by the Elders of the Night. The Ifá priests should also serve the Night for him.

He Made Divination for Odogbonikere:

Agbon losoo sibi hari hari. Okpe eluju lo gase logarun. Adifa fun Odogbonikere ti yio je ola edu ti ti ti. Mora eku lo ja, emi ko san wo, Odogbonikere. Ola edu laanje, Odogbonikere. Mo ra eja ati eran loja, mio san wo, Odogbonikere. Ola Ifá laanje. Mora'ya loja, mio san wo, Odogbonikere. Ola Ifá laanje, Odogbonikere.

The coconut tree bears fruits at a height the hand cannot reach, unaided. The palm tree has long legs and long neck. These were the benefits of Ifá throughout the span of his life. He was able to buy rat, fish, goat and a wife from the market without paying for any of them, because Odogbonikere came to the world to enjoy the fortunes and providence of Òrúnmìlà.

He made sacrifice with a goat and he enjoyed a prosperous life throughout. When this Odù appears at

Ugbodu, the person will be advised to serve Ifá well so that he will never be in want throughout his life. At divination, the person should be told to have his own Ifá, in order to enjoy a prosperous life.

The Special Features of Okonron-Oyeku:

Although Okonron-Oyeku was not a witch, he was nonetheless able to attend meetings held by the club of witchcraft. He was able to know how witches send out messages. He had a brother called Osogeregere. One night, his brother's matter was brought to the meeting of witches where they decided that Osogeregere should be given a basket to fetch water from the river. He was not to return until he succeeded in fetching water with the basket. Osogeregere was a rascally young man.

After hearing the impossible task earmarked for his brother by the Night, he could not reveal the information directly to him. He however called on him to go at once for divination about his own life. Osogeregere responded by refusing to go for divination because he had no problems whatsoever. He was however successfully persuaded to go and also to serve a secondary divinity called Olugbodo (Akobie in Bini), with seven yam tubers. He was told that whenever he was to make the sacrifice to Olugbodo, one barren woman would come to meet him at the shrine. He was told to advise the woman to buy a mother-goat to serve Olugbodo in order to have a child.

He performed the sacrifices. As he was actually offering sacrifice to Olugbodo, a woman came and he advised her to serve Olugbodo with a goat in order to have a child. The woman was herself a witch and she was the one who was appointed by the Night to carry out the sentence passed on Osogeregere. The woman however served Olugbodo and she became pregnant. She subsequently gave birth to a male child. The woman, who herself was to determine his fate in the witch world, refused to give him the basket to fetch water from the river.

When this Ifá appears at Ugbodu, the person will be told that there is a barren woman in his family, and there is a divinity in his family of which he is to be the priest. He should not refuse to serve as a priest of the divinity. He should serve Ògún three times before completing the Ifá ceremonies. He should also give a second he-goat to Èsù. At divination, the person should serve; Èsù with he-goat, and Ògún with a cock, to negate trouble from a relation.

Made Divination for the Statesman to Have Authority:

Teekeshe Awo omode. Teekasha Awo agbalagba.
Oku u kan kan ko de eji. Eeledaoye. Adifa
fun Baba gbobe korun, omo shan shan shan.
Ebodofin ru lana ofin shin shin shin.

Walk gently is the Awo of the youths.
Walk sharply is the Awo of the elders.
It remains one finger marking to become Oyeku-Meji.

These were the three Awos who made divination for the elder-statesman who accepted good advice to make sacrifice. After making the sacrifice his voice began to carry the weight of authority.

The sacrifice which the king made the previous day had already manifested.

When it appears as Ure at divination, the person will be told that he has recently made one sacrifice, which has been accepted by the higher powers. If it appears as Ayeo, he should be told that he has not made the sacrifice recently prescribed for him at divination. He should make it without any further delay.

He Reveals How Òrúnmìlà Left the World for Heaven:

Tee Keshe Keshe Awo omode.
Tee Kasha Kasha Awo agbalagba.
Okuu ka kan ko do oye.
Eleda oye Awo Ilare.
Adifa fun Òrúnmìlà, baba baa lo si ekpa
Okun ati ilaju osa. Onlo koni wa mo.
Woni tani won omaa kpeni baba. Eni ba tiri
Ki eekpe ni baba. Òrúnmìlà losi igbehin
Okun, koo ni wa mo.

The same Awos as in the preceding section also revealed how Òrúnmìlà left this world to join his fellow divinities in heaven. When he was leaving the world, Òrúnmìlà told his children and followers that he was leaving for the home beyond the sea for good, never to return. They came through the sea and he was going to return through the sea.

His children and followers asked him who they were thenceforth going to refer to as their father. In reply, he told them to refer to anyone they saw as their father, because he was already set to return to heaven never to return anymore.

This was how Òrúnmìlà authorized his followers to reveal the names of their Ifá to anyone professing to be an Ifá priest for translation. If you meet any Ifá priest, tell him the name of your Ifá because he might be able to tell you about it, what you have not previously heard from anyone else. It is not possible for one person to know all there is to know about Òrúnmìlà, lest the person will go mad.

If anyone therefore advises you not to disclose the name of your Ifá to any Babalawo, it is your signal that the adviser is a cheat. Avoid him.

Ono-Ifá for a Peaceful and Prosperous Life:

Òrúnmìlà ni Aronmo, Moni Aronmo
Oni ki a mu nkan ebo re wa.

Òrúnmìlà said Embrace.
I also said embrace.
He asked for the necessary sacrifice.

He declared the necessary materials for the sacrifice to be; shea butter (Ori-oyo) palm kernel oil (Adin in Yorùbá and Uden in Bini) palm oil, 16 snails, and the relevant Ifá leaves (Ewe-Orowo). He went on to remark that the palm oil seller embraces her wares. As soon as the sheer butter sets its eyes on fire, it must melt.

The snail never suffers a hot life, its life is ever cool and peaceful.

When all the foregoing materials are used for a special sacrifice, the person will obtain instant relief from all the difficulties previously besetting him. He will enjoy a heat-free life thereafter.

Divined for the people of Igbehin and Itori:

Itekiti Awo Omode. Itekara Awo agba.
O wa ku nkan kio de'ji oye.
Kole deji oye.

These were the Awos who made divination for the people of Igbehin and Itori. They were told to make sacrifice to abate the threat from death. They were required to make the sacrifice with a he-goat to Èsù and a ram to Ifá. The people of Igbehin made the sacrifice but those of Itori refused to make any sacrifice.

After being told by Ighoroko that the people of Itori refused to make sacrifice, Èsù rose up in the small hours of one night and danced from Igbehin to Itori with a drum in hand, to the accompaniment of the following incantational song:

Iku ti i ba pa ara Igbehin,
O lo pa won ni ode Itori, (twice)
Aro pele igi eni ju,
Ifá ba ro ibi leri ota.

The death that would have ravaged the people
of Igbehin,
Proceeded to plunder the people of Itori.
Peace be unto those who make sacrifice, by
Enabling Òrúnmìlà to save his people,
From the machinations of their enemies.

The following day, there was an epidemic of cholera in Itori which killed forty people in one fell swoop. Those who heard the song of Èsù in the night trooped to the Oloja of Itori to report the incident. Rather belatedly, the people of Irori made the sacrifice and there were no more deaths.

When this Ifá appears at divination, the person will be told to make sacrifice to checkmate the enemy who is contriving to kill him.

Chapter Three
Okonron-Iwori
Okonron-Kosi

```
I I   I I
 I    I I
 I    I I
I I    I
```

The Divination He Made Before Leaving Heaven:

This Odù came to the world at a time when it was still possible to shuttle between heaven and earth. Visitors to the earth were returning to heaven to tell stories of the strife on earth, such that people had to reflect deeply before embarking on a trip to the world. When it was his turn to visit the earth, he went for divination on what to do to have an easy time there. He went to an Awo called:

Mera ba o ni iri odele.
I will not be a victim of the mass death on earth.

The Awo told him that the world was at war and that unless he made sacrifice he might not be able to do anything to ameliorate its effects. He was advised to make sacrifice with; a Guinea-fowl to his head, and he-goat for Èsù-Obadara, (that is, the Èsù of the forest). He did the sacrifice.

On getting to the world, he met a number of elders who were pioneers on earth. He soon began to feel the tribulations of the world. In his own community, there were at least ten persons dying prematurely every day. When he discovered that there was virtually nothing he could do to arrest the situation, he decided to return to heaven for more in depth consultations. He went straight to his diviner, but the man was ill.

He however confirmed to him that the world was as horrifying as he predicted. The Awo told him to collect pieces of all edible materials and put them in a bag and hang it suspended on a tree in the forest, when he got back to earth. He did the sacrifice accordingly when he returned to earth.

After the sacrifice, he was able to save people from dying. When this Ifá appears at Ugbodu, the person should be told that he is supposed to be a practicing Ifá priest endowed with the power to bring salvation to suffering humanity. In addition to the normal Èsù for his Ifá, he should also prepare Èsù-Obadara for sending messages.

He Made Divination for the Rain in Heaven:

Okonron ri-ri-ri, Babaláwo ojo, odifa fun ojo.

He made divination for the Rain when he was preparing to come to the world. When he asked Rain what he was going to do on earth, he replied that he was going to bring good fortune to the inhabitants of the earth. He then advised him to make sacrifice with black soap, black cloth and black hen so that his benevolence might not be repaid with crass ingratitude. He however argued that there was no logic in asking a benefactor to make sacrifice so that his beneficiaries might appreciate his beneficiaries. On that ground he refused to make any sacrifice.

When he was preparing to come to the world, Èsù was told that Rain was going to the world without making the sacrifice prescribed at divination. On getting to earth, he extended his benevolence to; farms to yield good harvests, cool the atmosphere from the effect of heat and saved plants and animals from draughts. In spite of all the good work he did, Èsù had incited human beings against him. Those who were beaten by rain on their way from daily chores or prevented by rain from performing their daily chores, began to insult him for disturbing them. When the rain falls too often, people begin to mock him as an unwanted guest. When he is late in falling, people haul all manner of abuses on him for not coming to cool the atmosphere. When he comes, he is accused of disrupting their day.

No one ever seems to have on word of gratitude for the Rain, which made him to remember what he was told at divination. That is why he laments when he is coming out of black clouds:-

Bo ba je pe mo mo, ma ba rubo
Okan ri-ri-ri.

That is the signature tune of the rain when he is coming to the world as he continues to be vilified by all and sundry to this day.

When this Odù appears at divination, the person will be told that in spite of his magnanimity towards people, he is generally vilified and derided. He should make sacrifice to avoid continually being the victim of ingratitude.

He Made Divination for Fire:

Okonron wiri wiri wiri Babaláwo uno, odifa fun uno ni ojo ti aye uno re'le.

He made divination for Fire when his life was flagging. He was advised to make sacrifice with a cock, hen, and dried palm leaves. He made the sacrifice. His sacrifice manifested and he was reinvigorated. Iwarama Agbe aye uno dide. Whenever fire is about to extinguish, he can be revived with dried palm leaves.

When it appears at divination the person will be told to make sacrifice so that a light complexioned person might help him to prosper. If the divinee is a woman, she will be told that a fair complexioned man will marry her and make her life to assume great heights in prosperity.

He Made Divination for the Leper of Ijaye:

Okonron wiri wiri oriro teere, Awo inu ugbo. Adafa fun alakan ni Ijaye. Eni ti koo mo alakan ni ijaye, oun lofi igba re mu omi. Ebo ni ko ru o.

He made divination for the Leper of Ijaye. It is those who do not know the

Special Divination for Okonron-Iwori:

He used to make itinerant divination tours to several towns and villages, but had the spectacular weakness of being very forgetful. He was always forgetting his divination bag wherever he went. One day, he dreamt and saw a whole community of people beating him up. The following morning he consulted Ifá who gave him the green light to proceed on a tour he was contemplating, but that he should not quarrel with anybody during the journey. He was however to spread palm frond round his house before travelling so that all his previous losses might be recovered. He was also told to give; a cock to his Sàngó, he-goat to Èsù, and Guinea-fowl to his head. He made all the sacrifices.

Three days later; he received a message from the Oloja of Oja-Ajigbomekon a-kola, to come and save his life from a disease that afflicted him. He immediately proceeded on the journey. On getting there he discovered that he had forgotten the instruments he was to use for healing the Oloja at a town called Omuye. He was accompanied there to retrieve it. In actual fact it was invariably his divination bag that he had forgotten in the place. He had one medicine container inside the bag which he wanted to use for the Oloja. The medicine is capable of making the victim of any poison to vomit it. Apparently, the Oloja had been poisoned through his food.

As soon as he brought the medicine, he applied it on the Oloja and he began to vomit. The Oloja eventually became well. Since he had been ill for a long time during which several physicians and herbalists tried in vain to cure him, he appealed to Okonron-Kosi to settle down in the market town. He agreed to the suggestion, but asked for time to sort out his outstanding problems elsewhere. He was however later banished from the town when he tried to seduce the Oloja's wife.

When this Odù appears at Ugbodu, the person can be regarded as unreliable and very forgetful. He should serve; Èsù with a he-goat, and his head with Guinea-fowl so that his prosperity might consolidate. He should forbid anything bitter, such as bitterleaf and bitter kola. At divination, the person should serve Èsù with a he-goat so that his mind might not mislead him. He will also be advised not to boast in the presence of those who can help him.

Chapter Four
Okonron-Idi

```
 I     I I
I I    I I
I I    I I
 I      I
```

Divination Before Leaving Heaven:

When he was leaving heaven, his guardian angel told him to choose between relying on his physical strength and the practice ofIfism, on getting to the world. He was told to offer sacrifice to the divinity of Death in order to live long on earth. He was to do the sacrifice with he-goat, cudgel, and red cloth, but he refused to make it. In the alternative, he was advised to give he-goat to Èsù, but he could not be bothered. He made no sacrifice whatsoever. Rather, he boasted that neither Death nor Èsù could do anything to him.

As he was leaving heaven, both Death and Èsù dispatched malefactors to accompany him to earth. Death sent a man and Èsù sent a woman to follow him to the world. He became an Ifá priest on earth where he was always relying on the use of force. Contrary to the tenets of Ifism, he was using strong diabolical charms for killing those who offended him. It was not long before he met the woman sent to follow him by Èsù. She was a very pretty woman and he fell in love with her at first sight and lost no time in marrying her.

She became pregnant after the first month of meeting her and she subsequently gave birth to a male child who was the miscreant sent to him by Death. The son soon grew up to see that everybody feared his father. Nobody dared to face him. The son also grew to be a strong and fearsome young man who was eventually initiated to the king's palace society. Apparently, he felt so disgusted with his father's ferocious behavior that on a number of occasions he betrayed him by reporting to the Oba that his father was practicing human sacrifice. He disclosed that, Èsù had meanwhile quietly deposited severed human heads and bodies at the back of his house.

The Oba immediately sent for his father while simultaneously despatching a search party to investigate the allegation. The search party discovered two newly executed human bodies. They went to the Oba to confirm the allegation, although Okonron-Idi was not aware of the presence of the corpses on his premises. As he was leaving for the palace, he saw the corpses for the first time outside his house and he became spellbound.

When he got to the palace, the Oba accused him for engaging in human sacrifice and of ranking himself with the Oba. He was perplexed but denied the charges. Since he had no defense, the Oba passed the death sentence on him, and he was instantly tied up for execution. The Oba subsequently invited his son and told him that since he could betray his father the way he did, he was also capable of betraying him- the Oba. He too was sentenced to death by execution. Both father and son were executed on the same day.

When this Ifá appears at Ugbodu, the person should make sacrifice with the mud images of a man and a woman, a he-goat, red cloth and Ogun's scissors. He should serve Death with a cock, a chicken and a piece of red cloth at a road junction. This (Ono-Ifá) special sacrifice must be made without any delay so that:- the person might live long; his son might not kill him; and to avert the risk of committing murder or of having murder committed in his name. If he already had children, he should be told that one of them is eyeing him with morbid intentions.

How This Odù Solved the Problem of Untimely Death:

Òrúnmìlà ni ki Olokonron di'le,
Moni ki Olokonron di'le.

Òrúnmìlà told Okonron to close the hole on the ground.
I also, told Okonron to close the hole on the ground.

Òrúnmìlà said that the sacrifice for driving death away is done with a small chicken. (Oromu-adiye in Yorùbá) which cries Iku-ye-iku-ye ni Oromu adiye ma nke. With that cry the chicken is ordering death to disappear from the area, because Death forbids to hear the cry of the chicken. If a person is sick and is feared to be at the point of death, a live chicken should be tied to the shrine of Èsù to cry to death. Death will definitely leave the person alone.

He Made Divination for the Oro Masquerade:

Okonron dimu dimu made divination for the Oro masquerade when he was going to perform in the town of Egba. He was told to return home. He made sacrifice with a cutlass, broken fire wood, food and a ram in order to gain favors from the trip. He failed to make the second sacrifice with he-goat to enable him return home.

He was able to perform successfully in Egbaland. He also succeeded in helping barren women to become pregnant. He made; the poor to become prosperous, the hungry to get food to eat, and those suffering to obtain relief. His success made him popular and endeared to him so much that he could not even contemplate leaving the town.

He became an institution with his own secret Cult of Oro. Whenever the cult was operating, a curfew was declared after he has made an announcement:- Moti se ebo Okonron dimu dimu. That is the sound that heralds the curfew. Thereafter, women and non-initiates are required to disappear from the streets. His cult remains in Egbaland to this day.

When it appears at divination, the person will be told to make sacrifice before travelling in order to avoid becoming the victim of unintended consequences.

The Divination Made for Him When He Was Going to Buy a Slave:

Asa ninu esi bio ba leenka nkan maale bo na. Ofi igi gbo igi. Orisa omo ri giri giri sa'yo. Adafa fun Òrúnmìlà baba onlo ra mara Asa leru. Mara asa osa lo si ile Onidoko. Onidoko o ma sun menekun menekun. Òrúnmìlà o ma wa mara Asa lo si ile Onidoko. O wa ba ni be. Ara Onidoko ooya. Òrúnmìlà wa bere si toju re. Gbogbo ohun tiin she Onidoko, Òrúnmìlà she kuro lara re. Onidoko o bere si ko wo fun Òrúnmìlà, ati ashe owo fun Òrúnmìlà.

The Awos made divination for Òrúnmìlà when he went to buy a girl called Mara Asa, as a slave. He was told to buy the slave in order to prosper. On getting to the market he saw this girl as the only available slave for sale. He bought her and brought her home, but soon afterwards, she escaped to the house of Onidoko, who was not only ill, but had no settled life.

Òrúnmìlà traced the slave-girl up to Onidoko's house, but Onidoko told him that he kept her for him after she explained that he owned her. Onidoko took the opportunity to narrate his problems to Òrúnmìlà, who immediately began to address them. Òrúnmìlà succeeded not only in making him well but also in consolidating his life. He became very happy and compensated Òrúnmìlà elaborately with money and gifts in addition to surrendering his slave to him.

When this Odù appears for a man at divination he will be advised to have his own Ifá. If it appears for a woman she will be advised to marry an Ifá man or to persuade her husband to have his own Ifá, to enhance their mutual prosperity.

He Made Divination for Ògún and Sàngó:

He made divination for Ògún when he was going to learn how to cast materials from Sàngó. After Sàngó had taught Ògún for some time, that latter discovered that he had nothing to learn from the former. One day, Ògún asked Sàngó whether he was capable of producing any of the things he was teaching him. Adding metaphorically, Ògún explained that the reason he asked the question was because a needle must sew its' own cloth before sewing for others. In anger, Sàngó replied that if he knew so much more than himself, Ògún should leave his house.

Sango's only art was the moulding of mud images, while Ògún was capable of carving wood, casting metals and moulding in different kinds of materials. Ògún then challenged Sàngó to mould whatever he could for a contest with him in three days time.

Meanwhile, Sàngó moulded several abstract images and painted them with camwood. On his part, Ògún made a wood carving of the Oba of the town, as well as those of the two chiefs next in rank to the Oba. The carvings were like the real life sculptural representations of the three persons. Ògún then proposed that their competing art works should be sent to the palace for adjudication. When they got to the palace they threw away the mud images of Sàngó and hailed the work of Ògún. Ògún later accused Sàngó of moulding useless objects because he was ill.

Sàngó became annoyed and vowed to kill Ògún. Meanwhile, Ògún began to run from pillar to post. It was then he went to Òrúnmìlà for divination and he was told to make sacrifice with 7 needles, 7 snails, a goat and a he-goat in order to get Sàngó to become so paranoid as to get off his back. After Èsù had eaten his he-goat, he went to Sàngó to challenge him that if he was not stupid, what credit would a prospective Oba like himself (Sàngó was the heir apparent to the throne of the Aláàfín of Òyó) take for killing a small fly like Ògún. Èsù told him to stop moulding images and to start enjoying his princely disposition. Sàngó agreed with Èsù and left Ògún alone.

When the Ifá appears at Ugbodu, the person will be advised to serve; his head with Guinea-fowl, Ifá with a goat, and Èsù with a he-goat, so that he might prosper in his job. He should be told that there is someone stronger than himself in his street. At divination, the person should be told to serve Ògún with a cock and Èsù with a he-goat to avoid being sacked from his job.

Chapter Five
Okonron-Obara

```
 I      I I
I I     I I
I I     I I
I I      I
```

Made Divination for the Pounded Yam (Iyan):

Okon bam bam Awo Oniyan, Odifa fun Iyan ni ojo ti ko le orun bo wa si kole aye. He made divination for the pounded yam when he was coming from heaven. The pounded yam was told to make sacrifice with cock, white cloth, cutlass, fire flames and cudgel to avoid suffering in the hands of enemies on earth. He came to the world without making the sacrifice. When the yam got home from the farm, it was the cutlass with which he failed to make sacrifice that was used to chop him to pieces before being stacked in the pot and cooked on the fire. He was subsequently beaten to submission with piston and mortar before ending up in the bowels of human beings, the enemy he was told to avoid.

When the Odù appears at divination, the person should be told to make sacrifice in order to avoid suffering in the hands of human enemies. He should make sacrifice with; he-goat, white cloth, cudgels, fire flames, to Èsù and rabbit for the Night.

He Made Divination for the Mud (Atebo):

Okonron bar bar, Babaláwo Atebo, odifa fun atebo ni ojo ti kole orun bowa si kile aye.

He made divination for the mud used for building houses when he was coming from heaven. He was told to serve Èsù with he-goat in order to avoid running into difficulties with human beings. He refused to do the sacrifice. On getting to the world, he was trampled upon and beaten with both hands, by human beings before being used for building mud houses.

When it appears at divination for a woman, she will be advised to serve Èsù with he-goat to avoid the danger of marrying a man who will always be beating her, but from whose clutches she will not be able to escape. If it comes out for a man, he will be advised to take his own Ifá after serving Èsù with a he-goat in order to avoid incidence of crass ingratitude.

Divination Before Leaving Heaven:

Okiki ba ba ba ni merun okpokpo, was the Awo who made divination for this Odù when he was coming from heaven. He was told to make sacrifice in order to avoid the danger of behaving dishonorably on earth. He was told to serve Èsù with a he-goat, palm fruits, and the instrument used by secret cults for heralding a curfew. He was also told to serve his Ifá with a Guinea-fowl. He did the sacrifices before leaving for the world.

On getting to the world, his work was being derided by detractors and he was made a laughing stock. He became so despondent that he decided to go for divination where he was told to repeat the sacrifice he made in heaven. He did the sacrifice and his fortune turned for the better. He eventually became prosperous and popular.

He Made Divination for Oro, the Wife of Olofin:

The favorite wife of Olofin, called Oro, became the victim of a vicious falsehood. Her husband was told that she was being unfaithful, and Olofin believed the allegation, without giving her a chance to confirm or deny it. Olofin ordered her to be stripped naked and driven out of the palace in the nude. She took refuge with Òrúnmìlà requesting him to make divination for her.

He gave her clothes to wear, after which he went to Olofin to protest the manner of punishment given to his favorite wife, without investigating the allegations made against her. Òrúnmìlà told Olofin that the woman was innocent and appealed to him to take her back. The Olofin insisted that whether or not she was innocent, tradition stopped him from taking Oro back after sacking her naked from the palace. With that reminder, Okonron-Obara returned home.

At a subsequent divination she was required to make sacrifice for a better life, with a he-goat for Èsù. Knowing that she had no money for the sacrifice since she was expelled empty handed from the palace, Òrúnmìlà gave her all the requirements to for the sacrifice. He did the sacrifice for her. Meanwhile, they fell in love with each other and began to live as husband and wife.

Not long afterwards, there was a catastrophe at the palace of the Olofin and those who lied against Oro were forced to recant in open confessions. The cataclysm in the palace became so rife that the citizenry was beginning to wonder whether Olofin had not been too discredited to rule on the throne. As he got wind of the negative developments, he had to invite Òrúnmìlà for assistance. At a subsequent divination, he told the Olofin to serve Èsù with two he-goats, palm fruits and the instrument used by Oro cults for declaring curfews. He said that Èsù was annoyed because of the severity of the disdainful punishment meted out to Oro for and allegation that was probably false and vicious. He was also to serve Ifá with a ram. Òrúnmìlà made the sacrifices after which the Olofin formally surrendered Oro to him with full compensation. At the same time peace and quietude returned to the palace and the town after the sacrifices.

When this Odù appears at divination, the person should be told to make sacrifice to avoid becoming the innocent victim of a malicious falsehood.

He Divined for the Man Who Used to go to Heaven for Divination:

He made divination for the Awo who used to go to heaven to make divination, where his mother was assisting him. Each time his mother came to the market from heaven, he used to accompany her on her return journey to heaven. His mother used to tell him where to hide to avoid seeing his brothers who were also in heaven, but were plotting to kill him.

On one such occasion when he got to heaven, his mother told him to hide behind the mortar. His brothers later came to he house and no sooner they sat down that they felt the aura of earthly human presence in the house. When they asked their mother for an explanation, she put them off by attributing the strange earthly aroma to her physical interactions with human beings in the earthly market from which she was just returning.

The following day he went to perform his divination rounds after which he returned to earth from heaven. He was in the habit of boasting of being the only Awo capable of going to heaven to operate. His volubility soon brought him at odds with the divinity of Death, who began to wonder who it was that would come to collect divinational offerings from heaven to boast with on earth. The divinity of Death eventually decided to meet the garrulous man on earth. He combed the earth for the Awo but could not find him.

When he heard that Death was looking for him, he made divination and he was told to serve; Ifá with a ram, and Èsù with a he-goat, and to stop going to heaven. He made the sacrifices. After eating his he-goat Èsù made a rendezvous with Death and asked him what he wanted to do with the man he was looking for and he replied that he wanted to kill him. Èsù retorted that Death was being ungrateful for contemplating to kill a man who was always singing his (Death's) praise on earth. Èsù added that the man was always saying that heaven was a more peaceful home than earth. With those words, Death was successfully persuaded to leave the man alone and he returned to heaven.

When this Ifá appears at Ugbodu the person will be advised to serve; Ifá with a ram and two hens, Èsù with a he-goat after spreading palm fond on Èsù shrine. After slaughtering the he-goat for Èsù, the palm frond will be cut for the person to come out of the shrine, to mark his exit from heaven. He should forbid plantain and leaves called Malekpo. At divination, the person should offer he-goat to Èsù because of envy at his place of work. A stronger person is planning to kill him because of his exemplary performance on his job. He should resist the temptation to be voluble.

He Made Divination for the People of Otumoba:

Eshin ni ko ri oko gba.
Ojo ti a bi eshin ni eshin ti tobi.
Okuta ko ri orungbe.

The horse cannot find its way in the bush.
The horse grows big from the day it is born.
The rock has no place in the sun.

Those were the Awos who made divination for the people of Otumoba when unity eluded them. They were told to make sacrifice with 18 bats and 18 rabbits for them to be united again. They made the sacrifice. When making the sacrifice Òrúnmìlà recited the following incantation:-

Yams have to unite to constitute a barn.
The corn come forth not severally but jointly.
The sperm must fuse with the ovum to produce and offspring.

After the sacrifice, unity returned to the people of Otumoba. When it appears at divination the person will be told that there is no unity in his family. They should make sacrifice for unity to thrive among them.

Made Divination for the Calabash and the Melon:

Okonron Bakata, made divination for the calabash and the melon, both born of the same parents, when they were going to the farm at the beginning of the year. They were advised to make sacrifice in order to have children. They were also required to make a second sacrifice to stop enemies from devouring their children. They were told to make sacrifice with rabbit, a hen just about to lay, and cotton wool. They made the first sacrifice, but not the second one. Meanwhile, as soon as they began to have children, both human beings and animals began to eat up their children. The calabash ran back to Òrúnmìlà to make another divination on what to do to stop enemies from eating up her children. She was advised to make sacrifice with knife, baton, and sasswood (Obo in Yorùbá and Iyin in Bini). She made the sacrifice and the medicinal preparations (Ayajo) was used to rub her body, after which she returned to the farm.

When the calabash gave birth to a new set of children, Èsù warned their potential consumers not to eat them because they contained toxic substances. When people actually tried them they turned out to be very bitter. That was how the fruits and seeds of the calabash ceased to be edible substances, and hence how their mother brought salvation to them. The fruits and seeds of the melon, who did not make the second sacrifice have continued to be favorite alimentary items on the human and animal menu.

When this Odù appears at divination, the person will be advised to make these sacrifices to protect his or her children from being plundered by the Cult of Witchcraft.

Chapter Six
Okonron-Irosun

```
I     I I
I     I I
I I   I I
I I    I
```

The Divination He Made Before Leaving Heaven:

Okonron Kosun Lere, Okonron Kosin, were the Awos who made divination for Òrúnmìlà when he was coming from heaven. He was advised to make sacrifice with:- he-goat to Èsù, adding a piece of white cloth; red cock and a piece of red cloth to Sàngó; cock and a piece of black cloth to Ògún; and a goat to his guardian angel. He was required to do the sacrifice on account of the problems he was going to have from the people of the world. He did the sacrifices before leaving for earth, after being forewarned that his wife on earth would be a Sàngó the priestess, who had the key to his prosperity.

He got to the world and began to work as an Ifá priest. He was not erotically attracted by women for a long time. In fact, he did so much to shy away from any sensual relationship with women, that people began to wonder whether he was a complete man. Meanwhile, he travelled for Ifá practice to a village in Oyo where he met a priestess of the Sàngó divinity. The woman enchanted his masculinity so effectively that he lost no time in proposing marriage to her, to which she responded very favorably. After spending three days in the village he left for home. That was after obtaining clearance from the father of the woman to travel home with her.

Since no one in his home town ever expected him to get married, people were astonished to see him returning home with a wife. Many people came to welcome the woman, who watched them cautiously because many of them were Òrúnmìlà's enemies. As soon as the woman settled down, she advised Òrúnmìlà to go for divination because she had surmised the size of his problems. He subsequently invited an Awo called Akun Osun (the one who rubs camwood).

After divination Akun Osun told him to serve; his Ifá with a goat; Èsù with he-goat; Sàngó with cock; and Ògún with cock. He lost no time in making the sacrifices. His wife soon became pregnant, later giving birth to a male child. It was not long before he was able to build his own house. The wife also developed to become a very popular Sàngó priestess, who was divining for people every nine days, by possession. The family subsequently became very prosperous and he was given a chieftaincy title.

When this Ifá appears at Ugbodu, the person will marry a divine priestess, before coming within hailing distance of fame and fortune.

His Experience on Earth:

Before he got married, in addition to his work as an Ifá priest, he was also hunting on the sideline. He had a parrot who was often reporting on whoever called during his absence away from home. One day a woman visited the house during his absence and took a gourd of palm oil from the kitchen, without knowing that the parrot was watching her. She took the gourd of palm oil to Ògún-Esoto to add poison to it with a view to killing Òrúnmìlà. After inserting the toxic substances, the woman returned the gourd of poisoned palm oil to the house. The parrot watched all that transpired.

When he returned from the forest, he was about to use the palm oil when the parrot warned him not to touch it because a woman had come to take it away for some suspicious purpose before returning it. He decided to sound Ifá who told him to pour the oil on the shrine of Èsù, in addition to he-goat. After performing the sacrifice, her returned with his gun to the forest.

The vicious woman followed him without being seen, to the forest. When he subsequently took aim to shoot a deer, the gun exploded and the splinters hit the woman where she was hiding and she began to scream with pain. She later managed to leave the spot, but before getting home, one half of her body turned to a deer while the other half remained human. That was the deer he aimed to shoot in the forest.

The woman had been a widow for a long time and she had done everything to attract Òrúnmìlà to befriend her, but without success, because he was at the time not interested in any woman. After failing on that score, she decided to end Òrúnmìlà's life. She subsequently died from the injuries received from the bullets that strayed from the explosion of the gun.

When this Ifá appears at Ugbodu, the person should; serve his Ifá and head together with a goat, prepare Ògún for the Ifá with a cock, and serve Èsù with he-goat. He should forbid deer meat and rear a parrot. At divination the person should serve; Ògún with a cock, Èsù with he-goat, and Ifá with four snails.

He Made Divination for Òsanyìn, the Medicine Divinity:

Okonron kosun kosun, Awo ile Òrúnmìlà. Odifa fun Òsanyìn nijo to ti kole orun bowa si kole aiye.
He made divination for Òsanyìn (Osun in Bini) the Medicine divinity when he was coming to the world. He was advised to make sacrifice with he-goat, hen, rat and fish in order to avoid any leakage of his secrets while on earth. He made the sacrifice which explains why no one knows his secrets to this day.

When it appears at divination the person will be told that he is contemplating to do something on which he has some missing. He should be given the all clear to go ahead to do it, and the secret will never be revealed, provided he makes sacrifice.

Ori ewe ni mu oshe je subsequently made divination for Òsanyìn to become popular, effective and famous on earth. At divination the person should be told to have his own Ifá and to prepare Òsanyìn for it.

Divination for Wealth and Prosperity:

Òrúnmìlà said Ikosun.
I said Ikosun.

It is from Ikosun that people bring prosperity to the world. Only those who made sacrifice are able to bring fortune successfully from Ikosun to the world that enjoy opulence in life. The sacrifice is made with ipin and iyan plants and a mother-goat because it is "Ile kun keke ke" that the mother-goat cries, meaning, "the house is full of wealth."

When it appears at divination, the person will be told that his enemies are trying to destroy the good head he brought to the world. He should make sacrifice with a mother-goat and the Ifá priest will collect the leaves of the two plants, ipin and iyan, grind them together, and cook it into soup with salt, palm oil and the heart of the goat for the person to eat after adding the Iyerosun of this Odù. He will definitely prosper from that year.

Chapter Seven
Okonron-Owanrin

```
I I    I I
I I    I I
 I     I I
 I      I
```

Divination Made for Him Before Leaving Heaven:

When he was leaving heaven, his guardian angel warned him not to be too harsh and splenetic on earth lest he courted the risk of mental derangement and paranoia. His guardian angel advised him to make sacrifices to the following divinities:-

(i) Plenty of cowries, chalk, white cloth and pigeon to Olókun, the water divinity;
(ii) He-goat to Èsù:
(iii) Dog and cock to Ògún; and
(iv) Castrated he-goat to his Ifá and head together.

He did all the sacrifices after which he approached Ògún to accompany him to the world and Ògún agreed. On the other hand, Olókun refused to accompany him to the world.

When he got to the world he began to practice as an Ifá priest, but he was not very effective. His predictions and sacrifices were not materializing and manifesting, and so people stopped patronizing him. He subsequently became very poor. One night he had a dream in which his guardian angel advised him to go for divination. He approached other Awos who advised him to repeat the sacrifices he made in heaven as in paragraph one above. Since he could not finance the sacrifices, he had to borrow money to fund them.

Thereafter, he began to go for Ifá practice in the market place. By so doing, he was able to raise money to repay his debts. His Ifá practice had become more effective and clients were beginning to have confidence in him. One day, he saw Olokun's daughter in the market and professed love to her, but she rebuffed him on the ground that he was too abrasive for her taste. On getting home from the market in white apparels after giving another he-goat to Èsù. He did as he was told. The next time he made amorous overtures to Olokun's daughter she readily agreed to become his wife.

At the close of the market, she followed him home, and they began to live together as man and wife. Incidentally, for a long time she did not become pregnant. He again invited Awos to make divination for him and he was advised to serve Olókun with pigeon, white cloth, parrot's feather, chalk and cowries. He was also advised to serve Ògún with a dog. He made the sacrifices. Thereafter Olokun's daughter settled down and refrained from treating him derisively. She subsequently became pregnant and in the fullness of time gave birth to a male child called Money. She however continued her trading. Following the birth of the child, he became very prosperous and later married other wives and had several children. The first child became more famous that his parents.

When this Odù appears at Ugbodu, the person should be advised to develop a phlegmatic temper so that the wife who will make him prosperous may not be scared away through his mecurial temperament. He will give birth to a child who will bring fame and fortune to him provided he makes sacrifice.

He Later Founded His Own Town:

He prospered so elaborately that he was able to found his own town and became its Oba. In his town were two invalids, one had hernia and the other had throat tumor, and were next door neighbors. The two invalids were always quarrelling and coming for settlement before the Oba. Whenever the Oba asked them to narrate the cause of their quarrel, they often retorted by saying "ask the other". The Oba would advise them to stop quarrelling, but invariably they returned home only to drag themselves again to the palace the next day.

One day, the hernia patient, a man, and the tumor patient a woman, both dragged themselves once more to the palace. The tumor patient was wailing in tears. When asked why she was crying, she explained that the man was laughing at her affliction because it was exposed. When asked why he was laughing at the woman, he explained that she was the first to laugh at him with a problem he had in his stomach. His own affliction was effectively concealed under his clothes while the woman had no way of concealing her throat tumor. After pacifying them to return home the Oba appointed a palace detective to investigate the actual cause of the incessant quarrels.

The following morning the detective assuming a vantage position opposite their two houses from where he could watch developments. Not long afterwards, the hernia patient came out to sit in front of his house. A little later, the tumor patient also came out and sat in front of her house. The woman began by making a circle with her two hands in the position of her private part and the man reacted by demonstrating her tumor with his two hands to his throat. Instantly, the woman began to cry, and subsequently, they made once more for the palace.

When the detective reported his findings to the Oba, he decide to persuade them to stop laughing at each other. He however decided to make divination for them, after which he advised the man to serve his late father with a ram, which he was to kill single-handedly. The woman was also advised to serve her head alone with a hen without calling anybody.

They both thanked the Oba and went home to arrange for their respective sacrifices. As the man was struggling to kill the ram alone, it kicked its hind leg into his private part and it exploded the hernia and the pus began to ooze out. The accident made him to fall down, unconscious. By the time he regained consciousness, his hernia was gone. The same thing happened to the woman. As she too was trying to kill the hen with which she served her head, it pierced it toenails deep into her tumor and the pus trapped therein began to ooze out and she was relieved. The next morning both of them went in amity to express their gratitude to the Oba, who was happy to see the end of their quarrels.

When this Ifá appears at Ugbodu, the person will be advised to beware of someone suffering from hernia. He should serve his Ifá with a ram, give a he-goat to Èsù, and serve his head with a cock. His house is likely to be opposite that of a woman. At divination the person should serve; Ògún with a cock, and Èsù with he-goat, to avoid running into difficulties with neighbors or associates.

He Made Divination for the Dog:

Okonron wain wain, Babaláwo aja, odifa fun aja. He made divination for the dog, advising her to make sacrifice in order to have children. She was also told to make a second sacrifice to avoid incessant quarrels with her children after having them. She made the sacrifice to have children but failed to make the second one for avoiding internecine wrangling.

The result was that when the children grew up, and went their separate ways, anytime the children and their mother met, they were always fighting. That has become the peculiarity of the canine breed to this day.

When it appears at divination, the person should be told that he has a quarrelsome disposition. He should refrain from it.

Made Divination for Sàngó:

Okonron ajagbile, Babaláwo Sàngó, odifa fun Sàngó.

He made divination for Sàngó when he was coming to the world, advising him to make sacrifice. All the other divinities had complained that Sàngó was too aggressive and volatile, especially as he was always emitting fire from his mouth when he spoke. When the other divinities eventually ostracized him, he went to Òrúnmìlà for divination. He was advised to make sacrifice with a ram adding all eatables. He did the sacrifice after which the other divinities invited him for rapprochement and re-fraternization. He declined the invitation and they all trooped to his house where there was a reconciliation.

When the Odù appears at divination the person should be told to make sacrifice so that all his enemies might recant and become friendlier. For a man, he will soon have a new woman to marry. For a woman, a man of a different tribe will approach her for marriage. That is, if the divination indicates Ure. The sacrifice will be made with a goat for a man and a he-goat for a woman.

He Made Divination for Alapini Iyan-Iyan, and Ikola:

He made divination for Alapini Iyan-Iyan advising him to make sacrifice in order to avoid the danger of death. He was told to make sacrifice with a ram and his wearing apparel. He refused to make the sacrifice and he subsequently died suddenly. After his death, his children lay him in state and called on him:-

Alapini o.
Ti o ba se ki iku ni o ku,
Ki iwo fi gbi gbi je eni.
Ti o ba se si-sun ni o nsun,
Ki o tara je ni.
Alapini o.

Meaning:
If your death is natural,
May your soul rest in perfect peace
But if you are merely sleeping,
Then wake up like a man again.

When they called on him a second time, he answered by recalling the name of the Awo who made divination for him, adding that he had to stay with the people of heaven because of the sacrifice he refused to make.

At divination, the person should be told that an elderly man is about to die, which will make him (divinee) to spend a lot of money, unless he performs the above-mentioned sacrifice.

Chapter Eight
Okonron-Ogunda

```
I    I I
I    I I
I    I I
I I    I
```

He Made Divination for Animal-Kind and Divinities:

Okonron kogún kÒgún, Okonron kogbon kogbon. Aka i katan ni omode n ka ewe agboyin ni poro oko. Adifa fun eranko merindilojo.

The priest who interprets Ifá in twenty ways, the priest who interprets Ifá in thirty ways and the uncountable leaves of Agbonyin which children count endlessly in the bush, were the three Awos who made divination in heaven for 480 animals and 480 divinities. They were advised to make sacrifice to avoid the risk of starvation. Each kindred was told to make sacrifice with four cocks and cherry fruits (Agbalumo in Yorùbá and Otien in Bini.) The divinities made sacrifice but the animals refused.

Once upon a time, there was famine in heaven and everyone was looking for food to eat. The divinities made an appeal to God and He gave them the seeds of cherry tree (Osan Agbalumo in Yorùbá and Otien in Bini), which they immediately planted. Èsù soon blew air and water into the seeds, and within three days it had germinated. Within a span of ten days, it had yielded fruits and on seventeen days the fruits were ripe for plucking. The divinities subsequently began to feed on it.

Meanwhile, the he-goat was passing by the tree when he saw the ripe fruits fallen to the ground. He collected as many fruits as he could carry to feed his family at home. Thereafter, he made a point of visiting the foot of the tree every morning to collect fruits to feed his family. Not long afterwards, the divinities discovered that an intruder was visiting the tree to collect its fruits unauthorizedly. The divinities reacted by setting traps round the tree called Ibante Ojebeto in Yorùbá.

The next time the he-goat came to the tree, he was caught in the trap and he began to cry for help. When the divinities later discovered him in the trap, each of them began to foul the air (mess) on his head. The toxic gas from the fouled air killed him, and when the divinities asked among themselves who would eat the culprit, Èsù volunteered to take the he-goat. These two incidents explain why the head of the he-goat has an odor and why the he-goat remains the favorite food of Èsù to this day.

When the Odù appears at divination, the person will be advised to make sacrifice to prevent illness on the head. He should make sacrifice with he-goat and black soap. The blood of the he-goat and the soap will be used to wash the person's head on the shrine of Èsù.

If the divination is made by a community or group of people to find out the prospects for a particular year, they will be told to make sacrifice to avoid austerity throughout that year.

The Divination He Made Before Leaving Heaven:

Before leaving heaven, he made divination at which he was advised to serve Ògún with palm wine, cock, dog, and tortoise in order to avoid being killed by Ògún on earth. He was also to serve: Èsù with a he-goat, and his head and Ifá with a crocodile. He came to the world after making all the sacrifices and after receiving the blessing of God.

On getting to the world, he was being undermined by the elderly Awos, but when they discovered that his divination and sacrifices were manifestly efficacious, they began to watch him. Just as Òrúnmìlà expects his followers to do, whenever his divinees could not afford to fund expensive sacrifices, he would make-do with affordable improvisations (Aseboru). If for instance a divinee was required to make sacrifice with a Guinea-fowl, hen, cock and pigeon, goat or ram, he would ask them to fetch a chicken for blood, while using the feathers of the required birds and or the bones of the required animals, for the sacrifice, which often manifested as if live sacrificial victims were used. People began to flock to him which earned him the envy of other divine priests.

At meetings of divine priests he was often derided and despised and the Ògún priests were particularly up in arms against him. He later went for divination at which he was told to serve; Ògún with dog, cock, tortoise and gourd of palm wine, Èsù with he-goat, and Ifá with a crocodile. He did all the sacrifices after which his enemies left him in peace. He continued to enjoy popular acclaim on account of the effectiveness of his work. He was very prosperous.

When this Ifá appears at Ugbodu, the person should prepare Ògún for himself, so that no one would be able to harm him with Ògún. He will be successful in whatever work he does, but success will also generate enmity. At divination, the person should have his own Ifá and Ògún, or he should serve; Ifá with a crocodile and Èsù with a he-goat.

He Made Divination for Ògún and the Oraclist:

Before leaving heaven, he made divination for Ògún, advising him to make a feast for his guardian angel with fourteen different birds and animals, and to give he-goat to Èsù, in order to avoid becoming the thankless servant of all. He refused to make the sacrifice, which explains why Ògún later became the unappreciated servant of all divinities and mankind alike.

He also made divination for the Oraclist advising him to make sacrifice to God with white cloth, Opa atori (squirrel's stick or unwenriontan in Bini), white chalk, white kolanut and parrot's feather. He did the sacrifice after which God gave him the instrument of authority (ASE) for all his prediction to come true. That explains his popularity on getting to the world.

He Made Divination for Three Ifá Priests With Challenging Nick-Names:

Iwu lo fi ori arigbo she lie.
Ure la'fon kpe kokoro.
Akorko li gbena gbena ara-igi.
Awon meteta l'andifa fun ka-ki-lÒgún, Abufun
Ka ki logbon, atun bu fun egbe okpe to'on shomo
Ikeyin won lenje lenje. Aba kii lo'Ògún katun
kii lo ogbon bi fa ba ti gbeni oun ni awa ni ma ma.

The gray hair makes a home of an elderly person's head
The cricket blows the trumpet for the worms.
The woodpecker is the carver for all birds.

These were the three Awos who made divination for three Ifá priests that had challenging sobriquets; They were called:-

(i) I can interpret Ifá in twenty ways:
(ii) I can interpret Ifá in thirty ways; and
(iii) Whether you interpret Ifá in twenty or thirty ways, what is important is for divinees to derive satisfaction and salvation from the interpretation.

If the Odù appears at divination for a man, he will be advised to have his own Ifá. If he already has Ifá, he will be told to learn to practice Ifism. If it appears for a woman, she will be advised to marry an Ifá man or to encourage her husband to take his own Ifá for their mutual prosperity. In all cases, the divinee should be told to make sacrifice with pigeon, hen, akara and eko.

The Three Awos And a Fourth One Also Made Divination for the Ifá Man:

In addition to the three Awos mentioned in the last section, a fourth one joined them to make sacrifice for an Ifá man who was having doubts about the relevance of Òrúnmìlà in his life. The fourth Awo was called:
0
Be eshin baa yan layanju, olowo re l'on kesi.
When the horse is yawning repeatedly, it is calling on its jockey, rider or owner.

They advised the Ifá man not to discard his Ifá, but to take good care of it because Òrúnmìlà would save him from the hands of his enemies and bring him to the limelight of prosperity. He was told to make sacrifice with a duck and he did it. Thereafter he began to prosper.

He Made Divination for Eshi:

Okonron kan gun, Okonron kange, Awo eshi.
Odifa fun eshi ni jo to'nshe Awo lo si ode oyo.
Ani ki eshi ru bo. Oru ebo na.

He made divination for Eshi when he was going for Awo practice in Oyo. He was told to make sacrifice and he did. He was well received at Oyo, because Èsù had heralded his visit as an efficient Ifá priest. He was introduced to the Aláàfìn of Òyó, who honored him by giving him a man to be feeding him. The man was called Ogolo lo Oyo.

At divination for a man, he will be told that a woman who is not from his town, will come to marry him. For a woman, she will be told to expect a stranger who will propose marriage to her.

He Made Divination for Ajija (Eziza), the Wind Divinity:

One day, Okonron-Ogunrere went to the forest and saw a flock of colorful bush hens (Oyele in Yoruba and Ukorobozo in Bini) sleeping near the river. Unknown to him, Eziza who owned them sat close-by watching them. Oknoron-Ogunrere admired the birds so much that he was no inclined to shoot at them. He decided to return home with the intention of returning the next day with a net to catch some of them.

As he was preparing the net, Eziza came to him with his wife Eluene for divination. He asked Òrúnmìlà what he wanted to do with the net he was weaving, and he replied that he wanted to use it to catch some of the beautiful birds he saw in the bush the previous day. Eziza however told him that he did not come because of the birds but to make divination for his pregnant wife.

When Òrúnmìlà made divination, his own Odù come out and he told Eziza that he had not disclosed the actual reason for his visit, and that he was merely using his wife's pregnancy as a smoke screen. Eziza insisted that he came to find out how to ensure that his wife would have a safe delivery because that was his only worry at that material time. Òrúnmìlà subsequently assured him that his wife would have a safe delivery of a male child. He added however that Eziza would have to make sacrifice with six live bush hens. It was at that stage that Eziza disclosed that he was a bit concerned about his intentions towards his birds because he wanted all of them. He however promised to produce six for the sacrifice provided his wife could be guaranteed a safe delivery.

The following day Eziza brought the six birds and his wife successfully delivered a male child the same evening, and the child was named Ewegbemi.

When this Ifá appears at Ugbodu, the person will be give birth to a son who shall be named Ewegbemi, and who will be given the Eziza divinity to serve. He should serve Ifá with a goat if he has one or have his own Ifá, to avoid the danger of being killed on account of something belonging to him.

At divination the person should serve Èsù with a he-goat to avoid getting needlessly involved in someone else's trouble on account of his own belonging.

He Made Divination for the Two Babaras:

Igida, Igi se ori, won-ron-kon si-kon, were the three Awos who made divination for Babara senior and Babara junior who were always arguing between themselves. They were each advised to make sacrifice with he-goat, okro and maize. Babara senior was told to make the sacrifice to avert the risk of losing power to his junior. Nonetheless, he refused to make the sacrifice because he could not imagine how anyone could dare to usurp his authority. Babara junior however made the sacrifice.

In a subsequent contest, the junior Babara defeated Babara senior. That is why it is said in Yorùbá:

Babara bo Babara mo'le.
The young man floored the elderly man.

If it appears at divination, the prescribed sacrifice should be made hurriedly to avoid becoming the victim of unintended consequences. If the divination is for a group of people, they should be advised to make sacrifice to avoid losing authority to less privileged subordinates.

Chapter Nine
Okonron-Osa

```
I I    I I
I      I I
I      I I
I       I
```

Made Divination for the Guinea-fowl:

Okonron Konron ron ron. Odifa fun Aworo ugbo, to tori toma dafa. He made divination in heaven for the Guinea-fowl in order to have children. She was advised to make sacrifice with hen, rat, fish, akara and eko. She made the sacrifice and began to have children. Whenever she felt the approach of danger, she would shout the name of the Awo who made divination for her - moti she'bo Okonron kan ron ron ron-kan kan kan.

He Made Divination for Oya, Obalifon, Asa and Awodi:

Okan sa, Eji sa, odifa fun Oya ni jo ti o she Awo lo si ode ara. Abu fun Ogalifon on she Awo lol si ode Iyenden. Otun bu fun Asa ati Awodi.

He made divination in heaven for Oya when she was going for divine practice at Ata. He also made divination for Obalifon when he was going for Awo practice in the land of Iyendin. At the same time, he made divination for the Hawk and Awodi. He advised all four of them to make sacrifice and they all did each with a cock, a hen, three eggs and scissors (Emu in Yorùbá and Awan in Bini). That is why the missile thrown by each of them never misses target.

Divination for Prosperity:

>Mi'ra we wele, mi ugbo ru
>Mi'ra we wele, mi ule ru
>Bi ugbo ba ti ru, omo eronko aa de.
>Bi ule ba ti ru, omo araye aa de.
>Mi ira we wele, mi omi ru.
>Bi omi ba ti ru, omo eja aa de.

>When the forest blossoms, animals will flourish.
>When the house florishes, human beings will prosper.
>When the river profuses, fishes will multiply.

When this Odù appears at divination, the person will be told to perservere in his poverty because before the evening of his life, he will flourish, multiply and prosper, provided he makes sacrifice with cock, guinea-fowl, hen and eggs.

He Made Divination for the Snake in Heaven:

Okonron shale, sha okuta elasara, was the Awo who made divination for the snake. He was advised to make sacrifice to avoid intimidation. He was required to make sacrifice with Two Hundred needles, a cock and cotton wool. He made the sacrifice and he was told to carry it to Èsù. When he got to Èsù, he was told to open his mouth and Èsù lined his jaws with the needles. After spitting into the mouth of the snake, Èsù told him that whenever the needle touches any person or animal, the venom in the needle will not only sting the victim but line his bloodstream with morbid toxin. It was from then on that the snake became the fiendish reptile that his is today.

When it appears at divination, the person should be told to make sacrifice in order to be dreaded by his enemies.

The Divination Made for Him Before Leaving Heaven:

Uku soro soro ki aiba lu'le Awo.
Oyi fefe l'ongba ale orun tima tima.
Afefe era afe omo de udo afino.
Death cannot be strong enough to be met in an Ifá priests house.
It is the strong gale that sweeps the streets of heaven.
No wind can be strong enough to stop the kids of Udo from preparing fire.

These were the three Awos who made divination for Okonron-Osa when he was leaving heaven. He was advised to make sacrifice to insure himself against the risk of premature death, and to enjoy assured prosperity. He was required to make sacrifice with; black hen to Ifá, akara, eko, squashed yam and he-goat to Èsù, and to use a goat to make a feast for the police and youths of heaven. He made all the sacrifices before leaving for the world.

On getting to the world, he became an Ifá priest and after doing well for some time, he began to run into difficulties. He then went for divination and he was told to repeat the sacrifices he made in heaven. He made a feast for both youths and elders and they all prayed for him. At the subsequent meeting of all Ifá priests, he was appointed to be the one to carry all sacrifices to the unseen forces on earth such as the Night and Èsù. In the process, he became indispensable and prosperous.

He Made Divination for Sàngó and His House Help:

He made divination for Sàngó when he was travelling with his wife to dance at Omuwo. He was advised to serve his father with a ram, but he did not do the sacrifice. As he was dancing at Omuwo, he accidentally hit the eyes of one of his followers with his fingers and the man became blind. It was that man who used to prepare him for dancing and follow him about as he danced. After the man became blind Sàngó sacked him from his service The blind man later went to Okonron-Osa for divination. He was advised to serve his head with a cock, privately without the presence of anyone including his wife.

As he was praying to his head with the cock, it shot out its toe nails and it hit him on the eye, instantly removing the spider's web that beclouded his vision, thus restoring the use of his eyes. Okonron-Osa became so famous after that incident that at the subsequent meeting of the divine council of earthy, he was appointed by Arone to be the one to be carrying sacrificial offerings to heaven.

He Made Divination for Agbirari, the Friend of Èsù:

Agbe'bo ni o nsa gbure. Agberu ni o nsa gbure. Emu emuno ni o koko mo'le abe re nke reserese.

These were the three Awos who made divination for Agbirari, the friend of Èsù when he was hungry He was advised to go and hold on to his friend, Èsù. When he apprehended Èsù, the latter asked him what his problem was and he replied that he was always hungry. Realizing the utility value of his friend, Èsù proclaimed that from that day, if anyone made sacrifice without mentioning his (Agbirari's) name, he should seize the sacrifice and stop it from reaching its destination, including sacrifices to him, Èsù. In other words, no sacrifice will manifest without mentioning the name of Agbirari.

Before handing the sacrifice over to Okonron-Osa, the officiating Ifá priest should say:-

Kesu Agbirari
and then add
Okonronsa te te te, te te te, te te te.
adding the iyerosun.

Chapter Ten
Okonron-Etura

```
 I    I I
I I   I I
 I    I I
 I     I
```

He Made Divination for the Mouth:

Okonron tua tua tua, Babaláwo erun, odifa fun erun ni ojo ti erun t'onje aye ogbono ara. He made divination for the Mouth in order to over come the inconvenience of eating hot food. He told the Mouth to make sacrifice with eko and four snails. After the sacrifice, as the Mouth was sleeping in the night, Èsù line the walls of his stomach with the cool liquid from the snail with which he had made sacrifice. Thereafter, as soon as the Mouth ate anything hot, the snail liquid will be released to cool it down simultaneously.

When the Odù appears at divination if it is Ure, the person will be told that he is contemplating a difficult undertaking but that he should go ahead after making sacrifice with a hen and four snails. If it is Ayeo, he should give it up.

He Made Divination for the Hand, Throat, Stomach, Anus, Rubbish Dump, and the Sea:

Okonron tua tua tua, also made divination for the Hand, Throat, Stomach, Anus, Rubbish Dump (Etian in Yorùbá and Otiku in Bini) and the Sea or Olókun. He advised them to make sacrifice against the danger of unconsumated fortune (Amubo in Yorùbá and Osobe mo ma sunu in Bini). They were required to make sacrifice with a hen and four snails. All of them, except Olókun, the Water Divinity, refused to make the sacrifices.

Subsequently, each time the hand fetched food, he gave it to the mouth, who passed it through the throat to the stomach, who also passed it to the Anus, who in turn passed it to the rubbish dump or toilet and water or rain washed it all to the home of Olókun, who consumes it all.

That is why all the work done by the hand to fetch food for the mouth, pass through the esophagus via the throat to the stomach and through the anus to the rubbish dump or toilet, finally ending up through the porous soil to the underground aquifer into the sea or river. The work done by all the others who failed to make sacrifice to enrich Olókun, the Water Divinity, being the only one who made sacrifice

When this Odù appears at divination, the person should be advised to make sacrifice so that his efforts do not thanklessly go to benefit other people.

He Made Divination for the Harmattan:

Okonron tu tu tu tu, Awo oye doifa fun oye.

He made divination or the Harmattan, the cold dry wind from the north that blows in the tropics from December to March, when he was leaving heaven for the world. The masculine Rain, had proposed marriage to the feminine Harmattan, a beautiful woman, in heaven, but she declined his proposal The Rain continued to swoon her persistently but being the proud damsel she was, she continued to rebuff him. Eventually, she decided to escape to earth where she became very attractive and popular. She succeeded in putting both plants and animals under her command.

When her popularity on earth was reported in heaven, the Rain became annoyed and decided to meet her on earth. Before the interventions of the Rain came, the Harmattan had succeeded in defoliation the plants and humoring the animals. The insurge of the Rain was therefore a welcome relief on earth. The Rain drove Harmattan back to heaven and all the plants that had lost their foliage and glamour began to blossom once again.

When it appears at divination for a woman, she will be told to marry an Ifá man, because of the problems she is bound to have from a dark-complexioned man whose hands she would reject for marriage. For a man, he will be told that a dark complexioned woman is desirous of marrying him. He should accept her, provided he has or takes his own Ifá.

He Made Divination for the Dove:

Okonron tu tu tu, made divination for the Dove advising him to make sacrifice to save his wife from the danger of sudden death, which would make him weep. He refused to make the sacrifice. Not long afterwards, the wife died and he began to cry and to mourn, regretting that he should not have refused to make the sacrifice. He began to cry with the name of Okonron tu tu tu, who made divination for him. That is the cry of the male dove to this day.

When the Odù appears at divination, the person will be told not to tarry or procrastinate before making sacrifices recommended at divination, in order to forestall the danger of untimely death, to be caused by relations. The sacrifice is made with a goat and a piece of red cloth.

The Divination He Made Before Leaving Heaven:

Iya faa, Iya foo was the Awo who made divination for him before he left heaven. He was advised to make sacrifice with a whole bush goat (Edu in Yorùbá and Oguonziran in Bini) to Ifá and to give a he-goat to Èsù. He gave the he-goat to Èsù and began to look for the bush goat for Ifá. Subsequently, he was returning from the bush one day where he went to fetch leaves for his work, when he saw a hunter returning from the forest with a bush goat. He was happy to buy it at the asking price.

Thereafter, he invited the Ifá priest to serve his Ifá for him with the bush goat. After making the sacrifice, he left for the world, where he continued to practice as an Ifá priest. He was advised in heaven never to be too outspoken in the midst of more elderly Ifá priests. He was also advised to refrain from taking alcoholic drinks.

One day, he was at the conference of divine priests where he drank unreservedly. When he became tipsy, he began to boast of his capabilities and to reveal his closely guarded personal secrets. The elders became disillusioned with him and were at the point of using their ASE to curse him when Èsù reminded them that he was behaving unusually, because he was drunk since he was known to be characteristically reticent and taciturn.

When he subsequently became sober, he was told of his uncanny behavior when he was drunk for which profusely apologized to the elders. He went later for divination and he was told to serve: Ifá with a black goat and Èsù with a he-goat. He made the sacrifices with the help of the Awos and he was told to forbid drinking entirely. Thereafter he began to prosper.

When this Ifá appears at Ugbodu, the person should be advised never to drink at all and not to be too talkative at meetings and public gatherings.

Divination for Him to Have Children:

When he got married, his wife did not become pregnant for a long time. He tried everything he knew but to no avail. He also sought the assistance of other Ifá priests, but without any success. He finally went to an Awo called Aden who prepared the medicine that enabled the wife to become pregnant. He subsequently had several children but forgot to express his gratitude to the Ifá priest who helped him. That is why the children of this Odù are often called ingrates.

He even began to derive personal benefit from the medicine prepared for his wife by Aden, without giving any credit whatsoever to his benefactor. Whenever people approached him for medicine to have children, instead of directing them to the owner of the technology who had not formally transferred it to him, he would collect the relevant leaves that Aden used to make him have children, and prepare them for third parties. More often than not however, the medicine was not efficacious because the owner of its expertise did not willfully impart it to him. Since the medicine did not work, clients began to avoid him.

That was when he resorted to divination at which he was required to procure a goat and a hen to thank Aden. He made the presentation to Aden who thanked him without formally transferring the know-how of the medicine to him.

When this Ifá appears at Ugbodu, the person will be ungrateful to the Awo who prepared Ifá for him, which will create problems for him. He should serve; Èsù with a he-goat, and Ògún with a cock, and be told to forbid ripe plantain.

He Made Divination for Children Vying for the Throne of Their Father:

Boba kpe titi, Ifá a kpe Babalawo
Boba bu she gonjo Òsanyìn a kpe eleshigun
A tun kpe atoke kpelu re.
Ajoji Awo no wo oko kiri oyigi
Adafa fun won ni ile to maa gun ori oye baba r

After a while, Ifá will materialize for its diviner.
After a while, satisfaction will come to the follower and the leader in the Cult of the medicine divinity.

These were the Awos who made divination for the children who were contesting the throne of their departed father. They were advised to make sacrifice with he-goat to Èsù and a mother goat to Ifá.

The senior son refused to make the sacrifice and the most junior one did not see any point in wasting his hard-earned money to make sacrifice for a throne for which he was by tradition not qualified. The second son however made sacrifice. When the king makers eventually invited diviners to find out which of the princes would bring peace and prosperity to the society, the lot fell on the second son who made sacrifice. He was eventually made the Oba and peace and prosperity flourished throughout his reign.

He Made Divination for the People of Otu:

Okonron tu tu tu Babalawo won l'ode otu.
Odifa fun won l'ode otu, ti gbogbo won nusu ekun a lai no owo.
Ti won nsun ekun a lai ni obinrin.
Ti won nsun ekun a lai ni gbogbo ire.

He made divination for the people of Otu when they were craving for money, marriage and general prosperity. They were all advised to make sacrifice with a mother pig, sixteen snails and shea butter. They made sacrifice and all their desires were accomplished.

The place where the sacrifice was made came to be called Otu, on the precincts of Ife.

Chapter Eleven
Okonron-Irete

```
I    I I
I    I I
I I  I I
I    I
```

He Made divination for the Cockroach:

Okan re re re re, Babalawo anyinyan, odifa fun anyinyan. He made divination for the Cockroach, advising her to make sacrifice in order to obviate the danger of sudden death. She was to make the sacrifice with cane, rope, rat, and fish. She failed to do the sacrifice.

When the maid was sweeping the house one morning, she saw the cockroach and her many children. She killed some of the children with a broom and their mother fell outside the house on her back. Since cockroach cannot fly when it falls on its back, she began to call on the name of her Babalawo - Okan re re re re, while turning round in circles. Her cry attracted the fowl who killed her and ate her up.

When this Odù appears at divination, the person should be advised to make sacrifice to checkmate the risk of sudden death. The sacrifice is made with hen, rat, fish, rope and cane.

He made divination for the Boa snake:

Okon rete rete rete, Awo oka, odifa fun oka.

He made divination for the Boa snake (Oka in Yorùbá and Arunwoto in Bini). He was advised to make sacrifice against the danger of being killed with a stick by human beings. He did not do the sacrifice. Instead, he preferred to be hiding, not knowing that God had already appointed the squirrel as the crier to divulge his whereabouts to save other animals from his wicked stratagem. The announcement of the squirrel reporting the presence of the Boa is:-

Wa wo oka o elewu obobo.
Oka re o elewu obobo.
Oka wa mbi elewu obobo.
Oka ka ka ka ka ka.

by which he warns both mankind and other animals that the multicolored Boa is around. The declaration of the squirrel not only warns animals to run away from the area, but also attracts his main enemy, the human being. As soon as man hears the announcement of the squirrels, he cuts a stick with which to kill the Boa and he often succeeds in doing so because he does not escape from danger. The Boa only moves when his tail is touched by an unfortunate intruder, who often pays with his or her life.

When this Ifá appears at divination, the person will be told to make sacrifice to avoid being lied against by a person who is short and sharp.

He made divination for Water:

Okon re re Babaláwo omi. Odifa fun omi olojo ti awon meta mba omi she ota. Okele ge ge re ge maye ota omi l'on she. Ota pete, ota omi ni onshe. Gbongbo ibi mole segede si ona, ota omi ni o nshe.

He made divination for Water to triumph over its three deadly enemies:- the clouds of the sky; the rock and the protruding root-trunk of trees, who vowed to disrupt the life of Water by obstructing his movements. Thereafter Water found himself effectively engaged and he began to live in fear. One day, he decided to go to Òrúnmìlà for divination on what to do to overcome the inhibitive contrivances of his enemies. He was advised to make sacrifice with scarf (Oja in Yorùbá and Oza in Bini) he-goat, axe, bean pudding (Moin moin without oil) eko, pigeon, hoe, and cutlass. He made the sacrifice without delay.

Meanwhile there was a long drought during which Èsù had locked the rain tap of heaven. After eating his he-goat, Èsù opened the rain tap and the rain fell for three consecutive days. Èsù used the cutlass with which rain made the sacrifice to cut the clouds and the rain began to fall like it had never fallen before. All the rivers that had dried up became flooded. To combat the problem posed by the rock, Èsù used the hoe with which Water made sacrifice, to construct a by pass around the rock. Èsù also used the hoe and the axe to remove the root trunk of trees which had vowed to impede the advance of Water. With help of Èsù, Water was able to uproot the trees that blocked its way. Water then began to have a free thoroughfare.

When it appears at divination, the person will be told that he has three indomitable enemies who are sworn to blocking his prosperity. He should make sacrifice so that all their contrivances would come to naught, after which his prosperity would blossom.

Divined for Òrúnmìlà when Òsanyìn challenged him:

Oju ule okankan ewo eni ore.
Amaran ika ni itosi'gba.
Be eni ka ku, ni towo otun eni nshe.

The inmates of the house opposite one's house never look well at one.
The people of the house adjacent to the left of one's house never think well of one.
The people of the house adjacent to the right of one's house always wish death to one.

These were the names of the three Awos who made divination for Òrúnmìlà when Òsanyìn (Osun in Bini) the medicine divinity challenged Òrúnmìlà for seniority in heaven. Although, all the divinities were created at the same time by God, the frail and innocuous disposition of Òrúnmìlà tempted other divinities to taunt him from time to time. Òsanyìn boasted that as the magician that he is, he was more effective than Òrúnmìlà.

When God became bored with the incessant squabbles between the two divinities, He decided to settle the matter once and for all by putting them to the test. God directed Elenini, the obstacle divinity to test them. Elenini decided to lock the two of them up in a room for seven days without food or water, and that whichever of them survived unscathed, would be confirmed as the eternal superior. They were locked up instantaneously without being allowed to return home for any preparations.

On the third day, Òsanyìn began to beg to be released. Each time he wanted to cry, Òrúnmìlà would close his mouth with the advice that it was too early to bawl. By the time he got to the end of his tethers, no one could stop him anymore. He yelled out his capitulation by conceding eternal superiority and seniority to Òrúnmìlà. On the fourth day, Òsanyìn was released from the ordeal, but Òrúnmìlà refused to be released earlier that the end of the seven day span. He survived the seven days unscathed.

On the fourth day, Òsanyìn was released from the ordeal, but Òrúnmìlà refused to be released earlier than the end of the seven day span. He survived the seven days unscathed.

When he was released on the seventh day, Elenini congratulated him for the supremacy that Òsanyìn conceded to him. He did not conceal that fact that he was insulted. He proceeded to explain that after creation, he went to obtain two hundred and three different leaves from the Almighty God, and that he only taught Òsanyìn sixty one of the leaves, while keeping the mastery and know-how of the rest to himself. He then went on to query; how could Òsanyìn claim superiority when he only works with the 61 leaves he taught him, when he knew nothing about the remaining one hundred and forty two. He concluded by saying that an intelligent scholar was to be more circumspect and less swollenheaded.

At divination, the person should either make sacrifice with ram or he-goat in order to overcome his enemy, especially a junior person who claims supremacy over him.

The Divination He Made Before Leaving Heaven:

Ofi ohun ofia, was the Awo who made divination for this Odù when he was coming from heaven. He was advised to make sacrifice by serving; Ògún with a dog, tortoise, cock, a gourd of palm wine, palm frond and roasted yam, and Èsù with a he-goat. He was told that he was going to work closely with Ògún on earth, and so should keep him by his elbow, in order to prosper. He was also required to serve his head with a pigeon, and his guardian angel with a cock and hen. He made all the sacrifices before leaving for the world.

When he got to the world, he forgot to coalesce with Ògún, which made it difficult for him to have a settled life. It was when he was contemplating what to do with his life that his guardian angel ordered him in a dream to prepare his own Ògún, and to serve Èsù. A hunter soon befriended him, teaching him how to hunt. He also began to learn Ifá art and his fortunes began to change for the better. He soon became more proficient and more prosperous than the hunter who taught him how to hunt.

He Had Difficulty in Having Children:

When he eventually got married, his wife did not become pregnant for a long time. For that reason, he became a laughing stock. Whenever people asked for him, they described him with the derisive pseud-onym of "the childless Ifá priest." When he went for divination on what to do to have children, he was told to make sacrifice with a bird called Eye-Akoko.

For three years he scanned everywhere for the bird without success. He was subsequently told to go and look for it in the town of Akoko, which was inhabited only by women, because there was no males in the town. As soon as he arrived there, the women rejoiced and began to compete for his attention. He however told them that he did not come to the town in search of new wives but in search of a bird called Eye-Akoko to enable him to have a child. In reply the women said that they had long been looking for husbands and that having come to the town, he should settle down and mate with them.

When he sounded Ifá on what to do, he was told that the search for the bird that brought him to Akoko was an allegorical expediency for alleviating his problem of childlessness. Ifá gave him the all-clear to settle down in the town and to copulate with the women as far as he could. Thereafter, the women began to serve him in turns both conjugally and sensually. Within a period of eighteen months, he had twenty-eight children from different women, and before the end of three years he had close to one hundred children. He became the king of Akoko and his presence reassured other men to come and settle in the town.

At the end of the third year, he decided to make a thanksgiving sacrifice to Ifá, his head, and Èsù. He invited the Awo who made the last divination that brought him to Akoko, a man called Idagolo. He offered a ram to Ifá, a goat to his head and a he-goat to Èsù and he made an elaborate feast. When Idagolo came to see the many children of Okonron-Irete, he was so bewildered that he burst into tears. When he was asked why he was crying, he explained that the same Ifá that appeared for Okonron-Irete at divination had also much earlier appeared for him, but that he lacked the means of funding the required sacrifice.

At the end of his visit, as Idagolo was preparing to return home, his host gave him enough money to perform his own sacrifice. On getting home, he made the sacrifice and he too began to have children. In time he too became very prosperous.

The man for whom this Odù appears at Ugbodu will be a man of exemplary character and well behaved. He will leave the town where he got his Ifá to settle down in a new place close to a river or the sea. Three days after going into the secret conclave of initiation (Ugbodu) he should serve the new Ifá with another goat. He should also offer a he-goat to Èsù and be told to forbid a bird called Akoko.

At divination, the person should be told to serve his head with a Guinea-fowl, and offer gifts to the Water Divinity at the sea, on account of children and prosperity.

He Made Divination for the Man Who Married Olofin's Daughter:

Okonron were nle, made divination for his friend called Oyekunle, who was living with the daughter of Olofin without meeting her parents. After living with Oyekunle for three months, the princess proposed that he should accompany her home to meet her parents. Before deciding whether or not to go, he went to Okonron-Irete for divination at which he was advised to serve Èsù with a he-goat, kolanuts, a gourd of water, sugar cane, garden eggs and coconut.

After making the sacrifice, he was told to keep a bit of each of the sacrificial materials in his bag for the journey. He was warned not to fetch water or pluck any fruits on the way during his outward journey.

Two days after making the sacrifice, he set out with his wife for the journey to Ife. When they got to the first river on the way, the wife asked for water to drink. Contrary to her expectation that he would go to the river to fetch water for her, he brought out a gourd of water from his bag and gave her to drink. Next, they got to a farm containing garden egg plants having fruits. The wife asked him to pluck garden eggs for her, and he gave her from the ones he had in his bag. She did the same thing when they got to a sugar cane farm, a kolanut farm and a coconut farm. He gave each of them to her from his bag.

Unknown to Oyekunle but well known to the princess, stealing and lying carried the death penalty throughout the kingdom of Ife, and it was obvious that her demands during the journey were her secret stratagem for luring her innocent spouse to commit the offence of stealing having successfully lured two husbands to their deaths in a similar manner, before getting to Oyekunle.

Inspite of the fact that the man passed all the tests on the way, she had a final trump card to play against him. When they got to Ife, she introduced him as a most amicable husband, who answered to her beck and call throughout the journey. She went on to explain that; when she was thirsty on the way, he fetched her water from the river; when she became hungry, he plucked kolanuts, garden eggs, sugar cane and other fruits for her from the farms on the way.

Since her narration underscored a report that the man had been stealing on the way, he was instantly arrested and bound in chains. When he however denied the charges, Èsù influenced one of the elders to propose that verifiers should be sent to the custodians on the way to confirm the veracity of the princess's story. The elderly man reasoned that unless the princess was being deliberately mischievous, she should have warned a third husband about the fates of her two former husbands. The Èsù-influenced elder observed that it was reasonable to surmise that the princess was probably using the law to commit multiple murders.

When the verifiers got to each of the watchers on the route, they all confirmed that Oyekunle never touched whatever they were watching. They reported their findings accordingly, on getting home. The Èsù-influenced elder's premonition had been vindicated. After hearing the report of the verifiers, the council of chiefs formally invited the princess and accused her of lying. Since she had no defence, she was condemned for execution while Oyekunle was released immediately. The princess was executed in accordance with the law and traditions of the Ife Kingdom.

When this Odù appears at Ugbodu, the man should be advised never to marry from any royal family. He should also beware of any woman who professes love to him. In any event, he should make the sacrifice that Oyekunle made.

At divination the person should make sacrifice if he is proposing to travel, especially if he is accompanying someone else on a journey.

Chapter Twelve
Okonron-Eka
Okonron-Ala-Ayoka

```
I I    I I
  I    I I
I I    I I
I I      I
```

He Made Divination for the Ground:

Okonron eka sa kasa kasa. Babalawo Ile, fun Ile ni ojo ti ile minu iku. Won ni ki ile ru ebo. He made divination for the Ground when he was threatened by Death. He was advised to make sacrifice with hoe, cutlass, bow, brass, iron, and an old sheep. He made the sacrifice, which explains why the Ground neither falls ill nor dies.

When this Odù appears at divination, the person will be advised to make sacrifice for long life, in order to live to a ripe old age.

He Made Divination for the Mushroom:

Okonron awuka, Babalawo Olu, Odifa fun gbogbo Olu ti o mbe ni oko.

He made divination for all the Mushrooms in the farm. They were advised to make sacrifice both for a bright life and for a happy ending to their lives. They were required to make sacrifice with; white pigeon, white bean pudding (moin-moin) for a bright life, and a he-goat and their wearing apparels, for a happy ending to their lives. They made sacrifice for a bright life but not for a happy ending.

When the Mushrooms started germinating in the farm, they were very attractive and good looking. Èsù immediately alerted human beings to their nutrient value and they were cut down dead immediately. Those that escaped instant death, withered away within a couple of days as soon as they were exposed to the rays of the sun. That is why mushrooms do not live for more than forty eight hours.

At divination, the person will be advised to make sacrifice for a prosperous life and a happy ending. He should make the sacrifice without too much delay so that his prosperity might endure from the morning to the evening of his life. He should make the two sacrifices that the Mushrooms were advised to make.

He Made Divination for the Sun:

Okonron ribiti, Awo orun/ojo, odifa fun orun/ojo.

He made divination for the sun, advising him to make sacrifice with white cock, white pigeon, white cloth, and a broom. He made the sacrifice. After the sacrifice, he was given the broom to hold. He was advised that if anyone dared to stare at him on the face, he should stretch out the broom (rays) to dazzle the person's eyes. That is why it is impossible to look the sun on the face.

At divination, the person will be advised to make sacrifice in order to command the respect of the people around him. If the divinee is a woman, she will be advised to submit to her husband. The person should be told that he has one opening on the roof on his bedroom, through which he sees the appearance of day light. He should be told to cover the place because the elders of the night are watching his activities through it when sleeping.

He Made Divination for the Gourd:

Okonron ka ka ka, Awo Akeregbe, odifa akeregbe ni ojo ti 'onlo si aloro Odun. Abufun ugba, a tun bu fun ogiri.

He made divination for the gourd when he was going to the farm at the beginning of the farming year. He also divined for his other sisters, the calabash and the melon. He advised them to make sacrifice with black hen, club and machete. The gourd made sacrifice with chicken and club, without adding the cutlass and hen. Only the calabash made full sacrifice. The melon made no sacrifice at all.

They were all planted in the farm and bore many children. When it was time to harvest them, Èsù got up to compensate those who made sacrifice and to penalize those who failed to make sacrifice. He advised human beings to use chalk or charcoal to mark the calabash round its stomach and to cut it carefully so that it can be used as plate for eating or designed for ornamentation. The calabash plate was the first container used by man for eating and drinking. It is still being used for that purpose to this day. It has always been used and continues to be carved for decorative purposes.

On its part, Èsù directed human beings to cut the gourd at its top or by the mouth so that it can be used for fetching and storing liquid substances. That is why the gourd is used for carrying and storing water, palm wine and palm oil. It was also originally used in many communities for saving money.

On the other hand, Èsù told human being to use the cudgel to beat the melon and to cut it into pieces with cutlass to extract the seeds for consumption. Its seeds are used for egusi soup. Other types of melon are sliced into pieces and eaten as a fruit or dessert.

At divination, the person should be advised to make sacrifice to avoid being killed on account of his own possessions. If it appears as Ayeo, that is, foreboding danger, he should not try to intervene when people are fighting, to avoid being killed inadvertently or accidentally with a club or machete.

He Made Divination for the Bird Called Agbe:

Okonron ki, Okonron ko, Awo Agbe, odifa fun Agbe ni ojo ti on shawo lo si ekpa okun, ati ilaji osa.

He made divination for the red-feathered bird called Agbe in Yorùbá and Awe in Bini, when he was going for Awo practice by the beach area of the sea and at the embarkment of the Osa river. He was advised to make sacrifice with pigeon. He did the sacrifice and left for the journey.

On getting to these places, he had a lot of work to do for which he was handsomely compensated. His success was so remarkable that the colleagues he met at those places became envious, and plotted to make sure that he did not get home with his gifts. When he heard the boasting of his detractors, he collected his gifts and brazenly went home while they were fast asleep.

When he got home, he rejoiced and began to sing:-

mo de le koro koro koro, meaning

" I got home brazenly and safely with my gifts"

which is the cry of Agbe to this day.

At divination, the person will be told to make sacrifice before proceeding on a proposed journey, to avoid running into difficulties with other people who he is likely to outshine in the place.

The Divination He Made Before Leaving Heaven:

Okonron ka re le re, mi ko lo Okonron ka re, were the two Awos who made divination for this Odù when he was coming from heaven. He was advised to make sacrifice in order to succeed in whatever he did on earth and to avoid an untimely death through a woman. He was told to serve Èsù with three he-goats at the same time:- one he-goat was to be given to Èsù at home; the second one was to be given to Èsù in the bush; and the third one was to be used to serve Èsù in the river. He was also advised to serve Ògún with a cock, a dog, and tortoise after spreading palm frond on its shrine. He was finally required to approach the Almighty God for blessing with white cloth, white kolanut, white chalk, and parrot's feather before leaving heaven.

When he heard of the elaborate sacrifices he was required to make, he threw up his hands in despair, because he considered himself too poor to afford them. He however decided to approach God as directed and he received his blessing before setting out for the world. His guardian angel however warned him not to blame anyone for the inevitable consequences of leaving for earth without making the prescribed sacrifices. He left subsequently for the earth, coming out of the land of Ilara, the kingdom of Alara-Isa.

He did not take to Ifá practice but was trading and farming at the same time. As he was beginning to exhibit positive signs of making it, Èsù got up to let him know that nothing is ever got for free without making sacrifice for it. Èsù pushed him to fall in love with the beautiful daughter of a witch. The wife soon became pregnant and gave birth to a male child. His business was also doing well and he was never in want for money.

That was when he was suddenly taken ill. The illness refused to respond to any treatment and he soon became weak to perform any of his routine chores. The illness was procured for him through his wife and mother-in-law by the Elder of the Night. When he became totally bedridden and helpless, Èsù went to him in the guise of a sympathizer to ask him why he was not given to making divination. He replied that he had no time for fetish idolatry because he only knew how to pray to God for help. The man told him that God created people and also gave them the means of protecting themselves from the evil designs of malefactors, by assigning each person to one or the other divinity. He agreed that he was assigned to Òrúnmìlà, but insisted that since it was God who created Òrúnmìlà as his servant, it was more rewarding to revere and rely on the creator rather than his creature. Èsù gave up on him and left. Before leaving, he advised him to go for divination before he found himself between the devil and the bottomless precipice.

To mirror to him a clearsighted reflection of the fool's paradise in which he operated, he had a dream the following night in which his guardian angel projected to him a scenario in which with the help of her mother, his wife was packing and transferring his possessions to the witch world. Instead of arranging for divination on the dialogue he had the previous day with the intruding "sympathizer," he proceeded doggedly on his path of stubbornness and regarded his dream as a fantasy.

The following night, the same apparition repeated itself and that was when he realized that it was for real. He reacted foolishly by inviting his mother-in-law and his wife and flagrantly accusing them of bewitching him. An argument began, in which, at the instigation of Ògún, he mustered the physical strength to hit his mother-in-law.

The matter was re-echoed at that night's meeting of the council of witchcraft. Unknown to him, his mother-in-law was the queen of the council of witches and to have the audacity not only to call her a witch but also to attack her physically, was adjudged by the council members of witchcrafts as abominable. They decided that it would help him undeservedly to end his life painlessly. They decided to aggravate his illness before ending his life eventually. His sickness exacerbated and his wife left him. After spending all his money to try to cure himself, he committed suicide before his middle age.

When he got to heaven, his guardian angel reminded him of the warning to make sacrifice before leaving heaven. Since he had not exhausted his life span on earth, his guardian angel told him to make the required sacrifices and to return at once to earth. He returned subsequently to earth and the same wife came back to him. When he went for divination he was told to prepare his own Ògún which he did. He also had his own Ifá and became a practicing Ifá priest.

Once again, his wife began to transfer his belongings to the witch-world. In consequence, Ifá asked him to appeal to the ground divinity with a sheep because it is only the ground that can effectively chastise transgressing witches. He accordingly served the ground with a sheep.

Three months later, Ògún instigated an upheaval in the council of witchcraft, which induced them to start making open confessions. The Olofin ordered that they should all be sent for trial by ordeal, during which all of them including his wife, died. From then on, he settled down to a prosperous life and lived happily to a ripe old age.

When this Ifá appears at Ugbodu, the person should be told to make sacrifice. He has probably been a Christian before being advised to have his Ifá. His Christianity should not be disturbed by his Ifá lineage and he should be warned never to find out a woman's antecedents through divination before marrying her. He should be careful not to fall out with his mother-in-law. At divination, the person should be advised to have his own Ifá, and if he already has one, not to throw it away after embracing another faith. He should make sacrifice to the Elders of the Night.

His Work as an Ifá Priest in his Second Life:
He Restored the Eyes of the Blind:

He made divination for the people of Ilu-Omi, the land of water where so many people were blind.

When he got to the town, he made divination for them and he promised to do his best for their blind population, if they would make sacrifice to Èsù. He explained that it was necessary to make the sacrifice, because it was with the help of Èsù alone that they could find the two leaves he required for treating the blind. They agreed to make the sacrifice without delay.

Thereafter, he told them to look for the leaf with which a bird called Elulu in Yorùbá and Erumohi in Bini, opens the children's eyes after they are born. Secondly, they were to look for the leaf with which the male snake revives its female partner after making love to her. By the usage of the serpents's kindred, no snake can have sex with its female partner without first poisoning her into comatose. After making love to her the male snake plucks this particular leaf and applies it to her eyes to regain consciousness.

The king instructed the town's most proficient hunters to go into the forest to fetch the two leaves. Three days later they succeeded in obtaining them. He mixed the leaves with the divination powder of the opposite Odù and applied it to the eyes of all the blind people before they went to sleep in the night. The following morning, they all woke up with their sight restored. It was regarded as an epoch-making miracle and his fame soon spread around. He was rewarded with human and material gifts that translated him into eternal affluence.

When this Ifá appears at Ugbodu, the person will be advised to serve Èsù at once and to arrange to settle down to a new life near the sea in order to become prosperous. At divination, the person should serve Èsù with a he-goat and Ògún with a cock in order to receive an upcoming material favor.

Chapter Thirteen
Okonron-Eturukpon

```
I I    I I
I I    I I
 I     I I
I I     I
```

He Made Divination for the Horse:

Okonron Turukpon Babaláwo eshi, odifa fun eshi. Oni ki eshin ru ebo ni to ri kpe ki o ma be kpon omolomo, ki o ma ba fi ti ara re si ' le. He made divination for the Horse in heaven, advising her to make sacrifice to avoid the abject indignity of backing other people's children instead of her own. She was required to make the sacrifice with a hen, a rabbit and her own apparel. She refused to make the sacrifice. That is why the kindred of horses became eternally condemned to become beasts of burden, carrying other people's children on their backs, but never their own children.

When this Odù appears at divination, the person will be advised to make sacrifice to avoid the danger of having to care for the children of other people without having his or her own to care for. For a woman, she should be warned never to back anybody's child before she becomes pregnant.

He Made Divination for Onidiro in Heaven:

Okonron tu ka tuyele odifa fun Onidiro aya Òrúnmìlà ni ojo ti onkpa uro fun oko re.

He made divination for Onidiro, the wife of Òrúnmìlà when she lied to her husband. She had been flirting around with other men and Òrúnmìlà knew about her infidelity. When he asked her, she lied that she had never contemplated that sort of behavior.

After enumerating to her the number of men she had been cohabiting with, Òrúnmìlà pointed his staff of authority at her and he cursed her that from then on, she would be the one with which would always serve his head from time to time. Onidiro is the heavenly name of the hen, who was originally Òrúnmìlà's wife, before being turned into a hen.

When it appears at divination for a woman, she will be told not to be unfaithful to her husband to avoid being cursed. If the divinee is a man he will be told to resist the temptation to be deceitful to his partner, because his reaction will culminate in his becoming a pale reflection on himself.

The Divination He Made Before Leaving Heaven:

He was given the nickname of Okonron tutu the trader. He also wanted to come to the world to trade. At the divination he made before coming to the world, he was advised to made the following sacrifices, to:-

(i) Serve Èsù with a he-goat;
(ii) Serve his head and guardian angel with rat, eagle and vulture;

(iii) Serve the three-road junction with 4 pigeons, and white cloth and for the Ifá priest to bathe him on the spot;
(iv) Obtain God's blessing with white pigeon, white cloth, white chalk and red parrot's feather and;
(v) Serve Olókun with one of the pigeons in (iii)

He was told to serve Èsù first so that he can help him to obtain the eagle and the vulture for (ii) above. After serving Èsù, he also served Ògún with a dog. Thereafter, Èsù persuaded the eagle to fly to lower heights where food was available. Meanwhile, Èsù had also persuaded Ògún the hunter to prepare to shoot the eagle. As the eagle was eating ripe plantain in a farm, the hunter shot him and sold him to Okonron-tutu. Èsù also persuaded the hunter to shoot the vulture by the side of the sea and also sold it to Okonron-tutu. Thereafter, Ògún, the hunter, developed a cold because he was not used to operating by the side of the sea. Òrúnmìlà however prepared fire for Ògún and gave him a tortoise after which he became well.

After obtaining the eagle and the vulture, Okonron-tutu added a rat and made the sacrifice to his head and guardian angel. He subsequently made the other sacrifices and appealed to Olókun to follow him to the world. Olókun declined to go himself, but promised to send someone to accompany him, provided he would not neglect the person on earth. He eventually left for the world in the company of Olokun's representative.

On getting to the world, the two of them went their separate ways, and could not recognize each other. Okonron-Eturukpon became a trader but he was not doing particularly well in that vocation. He could not even afford to marry a wife. Olokun's representative, having strayed from the path of her assigned destiny, was also loafing about listlessly. Meanwhile, Okonron-tutu decided to go for divination, where he was advised to make sacrifice to Èsù, Ifá and his head. The Awos prepared a medicine in a calabash and bathed him in the river. Thereafter he continued with his trading.

He was trading in coral beads in the market. The next time he got to the market after making sacrifice, Olokun's representative was attracted by the beads he was selling but had no money to buy. She too had gone for divination on what to do to get a suitable man to marry. She was advised that her rightful husband was an Awo but to make sacrifice with he-goat, beads and pigeon in order to meet him. She had served Èsù with a he-goat before coming to the market to buy pigeon and beads to serve her head, all of which Okonron-tutu was selling.

As soon as he saw her, he took fancy to her and she was equally attracted to him. When Òrúnmìlà told her the prices of what she wanted to buy, she reiterated that she lacked the money for them.

Òrúnmìlà however persuaded her to come home with him to make the sacrifice. On getting home with her, he brought out a pigeon and bead to serve her head. Since tradition did not allow her to go out after serving her head and guardian angel, she had to spend the night with Òrúnmìlà. In the night, they slept together and copulated.

That night, Òrúnmìlà had a dream in which Olókun admonished him for not linking up earlier with the representative he sent to accompany him to earth. The water divinity confirmed to him that the woman he was sleeping with was his chosen representative who at his request, accompanied him to earth. Olókun confirmed that she was his destined wife but that he should make sacrifice to him (Olókun) with a pigeon, white chalk, cowries, parrot's feather, and all the materials usually sent as gifts to the sea.

When he woke up the following morning, he sounded Ifá who confirmed that the dream was a true-to-life reflection of his situation and that he was to comply with the directives he had in the dream. Without any further hesitation he took the woman to wife and she soon became pregnant. Prosperity subsequently flowed into his trading and they were ever so happy and wealthy.

When it appears at Ugbodu, the person should be told to prepare Olókun for his Ifá. If he is not yet married, the next woman he comes across is his destined wife. If he is already married, he is likely to come across the daughter of Olókun after the Ifá initiation ceremony. At divination, the person should serve Èsù with a he-goat and send the traditional gifts with a pigeon to the sea or river because of an upcoming gift from Olókun.

He Made Divination for a Seductive Basket Weaver:

One day, a woman called Beje sent her daughter to buy a basket from the basket weaver. When he asked who sent her, she replied that it was her mother. He insisted that if the mother truly wanted to buy a basket, she should come and choose one and negotiate its price by herself.

The woman, eventually came by herself and she bought the basket on credit. When he later went to demand payment of the debt, their discussions centered on amorous relationship which culminated in Beje agreeing to marry the basket weaver.

It was at that point, after consenting to marry Beje, that he went to Okonron-Eturukpon for divination. The diviner advised him not to marry the woman because her husband, who was a cripple, would create tremendous problems for him. If on the other hand he was bent on going ahead with the marriage, Ifá advised him to make prior sacrifice with ram. Without making the sacrifice however, he proceeded to consummate the marriage, because he could not anticipate any problem from a cripple.

Beje was not living with her crippled husband, but she used to send food to him regularly at the place where he lived. Meanwhile, Beje moved to live with Dehinde, the basket weaver. When the time came for the cripple to have his food, none was forthcoming. After wondering for long about what might have happened, the cripple crawled to the wife's house only to be told by his daughter that her mother had packed out of the house to live with a basket weaver. The cripple then asked his daughter to take him to the house of the basket weaver.

When he got to the seducer's house, the cripple demanded the return of his wife, but Mr. Dehinde reacted by telling him to go to blazes and roast to ashes, after calling him "You dirty cripple, do you have a wife? Get out of my house." Beje was in but did not know what was happening. When she was subsequently told what had happened, Dehinde was astonished when she confirmed that the cripple was her former husband.

The cripple left the basket weaver's house to lodge a complaint at the Oba's palace. He left the Oba with the impression that he was going to commit suicide on account of what Dehinde did to him. The Oba however persuaded him not to do anything stupid and to give him a chance to redress the wrong done to him. Before he left the palace, the Oba gave orders that Dehinde should be brought to the palace in chains.

At his subsequent trial, he was accused of inhuman behavior to his helpless fellow man, for which he was sentenced to death by execution. While he was being kept in detention awaiting execution, he remembered the sacrifice he failed to make. He begged the girl who came to serve him food to go to his house and tell his family to go to Òrúnmìlà to make the sacrifice, albeit belatedly.

The sacrifice was made and Òrúnmìlà gave them the head of the sacrificial ram to rub his head with the blood in captivity. Meanwhile, Beje had returned to her crippled husband. When the day came for his execution, Èsù influenced the members of the Oba's council to prevail on him to spare the man's life, since he explained that he never knew that the woman was married to anyone. They argued that the real culprit was not the accused, but the woman, who failed to disclose to him that she had a husband with whom she was not living. The Oba accepted the advice of his counselors and changed the verdict from death to perpetual exile which banned him from ever returning to the town. He was subsequently released and instantly banished.

At Ugbodu, the person should make sacrifice to avoid being banished from his town on account of a woman, serve Ifá with a ram, a hen and four snails; and serve Èsù with he-goat. At divination, the person should serve Ifá with a hen and Èsù with he-goat to avoid getting into trouble because of a woman.

Divination Made for Him Before Becoming Prosperous:

Aji tuu ru, Ela tuuru. Adifa fun Òrúnmìlà baba aofi omi oju shu bere aje tuuru tu.

Those were the two Awos who made divination for Òrúnmìlà when he was anxious for prosperity. He was told to make sacrifice with four pigeons, a cock, a rabbit and four snails. He made the sacrifice. Thereafter wealth began to flow into his home from every direction.

This is the special sacrifice which the children of this Odù should make in order to become prosperous.

Erukuku de, omo onishewe
Ese rere ni erukuku ma n fi te'le.
Ireku-Ireku ni eyele ma n ke.

The pigeon is a fetcher of prosperity,
By flying fortune into the house,
with its left and right wings, and by
crying Ireku Ireku, heralding the arrival
of wealth.
The cock requires no ceremony before marrying,
No rabbit comes to the world to become barren.
The snail lives a cool life and not a hot one.

If this sacrifice is made, the person will surely have money, wife, house and children. Whatever he sets his hands on must invariably succeed.

Chapter Fourteen
Okonron-Seke
Okonron-Ose
Okonron-Da-Ase

```
    I      I I
   I I     I I
    I      I I
   I I      I
```

Divined for Poverty, Suffering and Deprivation:

Ushe lo tan ishe. Oshi lo gbaagba taa re. Oni kpanju lo gba owo re na.
Adafa fun ushe, abu fun Uya, atun bu fun oro to nshe omo ikeyin won lenje lenje.

Hard work or effort terminates poverty.
The deprived person sells the wares of the pauper for him.
The vindictive person seizes the product of effort.

These were the three Awos who made divination for Poverty, Suffering and Prosperity, the last born of their parents. All three of them were advised to make sacrifice in order to have eternal honor and dignity. The first two of the three brothers boasted that far from desiring to have honor and respect, they preferred to be feared by God's creatures, and hence, refused to make the sacrifice. It was only prosperity that made sacrifice because he preferred to have contented followership. After an uneasy beginning, prosperity flourished later in life.

That is why people dread the onset of poverty, and suffering, while everyone longs for prosperity, who easily became the most successful of the three brothers.

When it appears at divination, the person will be told to make sacrifice for the accomplishment of his aspirations and desires. He will be reassured that the morning of his life might be interlaced with destitution but the late afternoon and evening will bring contentment.

Made Divination for the Snake When He Was Befriending the Squirrel:

Okonron seke seke, odifa fun Ejo ti o mba Akerese nshe ore.
Oni iwo ejo ru ebo to ri pe ti ki ore-re yi o ma ba'ko ba o.

He made divination for the snake when he was befriending the squirrel. He was advised to make sacrifice to avoid the risk of being betrayed and goaded into trouble by this friend the squirrel. He was told to make sacrifice with his wearing apparel, cutless, stick and a cock. He refused to make the sacrifice because he trusted his friend too faithfully to imagine any trouble sourcing through or from him.

When Èsù was subsequently informed by his friend Ighoroko that the snake refused to make sacrifice, he (Èsù) instigated the squirrel to start yelling at the snake where he was resting quietly. The squirrel began to remind the snake that he did not make the sacrifice that Òrúnmìlà advised him to make, by saying:

Iwo ko she ebo Okonron seke-re-kere.

Almost simultaneously Èsù drew attention of passersby to the presence of the snake at the point where the squirrel was yelling. The people cut a stick which they used to behead the snake, after clearing the surrounding shrub, with their cutlass. That death call remain the traditional cry of the squirrel to the present day.

When the Ifá appears at Ugbodu or divination the person will be advised not have rely too faithfully on friends. He or she should make sacrifice to avoid the danger of getting into trouble, which could be fatal, through the machinations of a very intimate friend.

He Made Similar Divination for Akinla:

Ajé ma gbe ohun mi lo si idi.
Ebora ma gbe ohun mi lo si orun.
Alaisan ma fi ohun mi li enu lo si ode orun.
Awon meteta l'ondifa fun Akinla. Woni ki Akinla,
ru ebo ni tori wi pe ki eni kan ma ba ke egbe re,
titi lo si orun. Akinla ko tete ru ebo na. Bayi ni
alaisan yi bere si ke igbe Akinla. Akinla wa sare ru ebo.

Witch, do not carry my words to the meeting of witches.
Divinity, do not carry my words to heaven.
Invalid, do not shout my name to high heaven.

These were the Ifá priests that made divination for Akinla when he was advised to make sacrifice so that detractors might not make a death call on him towards heaven. He was told to make the sacrifice with broken calabash (Akufo Igba in Yorùbá) and cock. He dawdled before making the sacrifice.

Meanwhile, an invalid began to sing with the name of Akinla as if he wanted Akinla to relieve him of the burden of death that was already gunning for himself. When Akinla's attention was invited to the death call being made on him by the sick man, he hurriedly proceeded to make the sacrifice. After preparing the sacrifice, Akinla was directed by Ifá priests to put it on top of a fence and to leave it to fall over to the other side of it. The impact of the sacrifice on the ground made a loud noise, wo! wo!

When the sick man heard the noise, he shouted to ask what it was that made the wo! wo! sound. He went subsequently into a stupor and began to shout wo! wo! wo! until he gave up the ghost.

As soon as the invalid died, Akinla began to rejoice and to sing in praise of the Awos who made divination and sacrifice for him.

When this Odù appears at divination, the person will be advised to make to make sacrifice to prevent anyone from putting death on his trail, or not to get into trouble.

The Divination Made for Odogbomukere and Okonron-da-ase:

He is regarded as a fay because he ran away from heaven. Before leaving however he made divination with two Awos called:-

Agbon o ro hai ka'ri
Okpolo l'onshe te re timu timu.

They made divination for Odogbomukere and also for Okonron-da-ase before they left heaven. Okonron-da-ase was advised to make sacrifice to; his head and guardian angel with a goat, pay homage to God with 2 white pigeons, a piece of white cloth, 20 red parrot's feathers, white and red kolanuts, in addition to giving a he-goat to Èsù. Since he did not wish to stay long on earth, he saw no point in making the sacrifice. He left for the world without making sacrifice and came out of Benin, in the Edo state of Nigeria.

He was very humble and respectful which made him very popular. He was an itinerant dancer, but on account of his humane and cheerful disposition, the Oba of Benin was contemplating to give him a chieftancy title. He was however heavily in debt because money was never staying with him. He was also very sickly. In spite of his popularity people began to wonder why he was unable to make ends meet. He was subsequently advised to go for divination, at which he was told that his problems arose from his refusal to make sacrifice before before leaving heaven.

He was again advised to make sacrifice to Ifá and his head with goat, rat, fish, tortoise, pigeon and hen, and to make a feast with the materials. He was also to serve his guardian angel with a pigeon, piece of white cloth, white and red kolanuts and red parrot's feather. He was also required to pay homage to God with a pigeon, piece of white cloth, red and white kolanuts and 20 red parrot's feathers. He was to use these sacrifices to buy long life and prosperity on earth. Moreover he was to use a three year old he-goat to serve Èsù and to serve Ògún with dog, cock and tortoise.

When he told the Ifá diviner that he had no money for the sacrifice, the man advised him to buy the materials on credit because if he failed to make them, his days on earth were numbered.

He met a sympathetic old woman who agreed to sell all the materials to him on credit. He came home with them to make the sacrifice. Soon after making the sacrifices, his fortunes took a better turn. After enjoying his sacrifice, Èsù went to the Oba of Benin and proposed to him that Okonron-da-ase was ripe for chieftancy title. He was made a chief and put in charge of all the markets. He was subsequently able to repay the debts with which he funded his sacrifices and he lived in prosperity to a ripe old age.

When this Ifá appears at Ugbodu, the sacrifices referred to above are the special sacrifices (Ono-Ifá or Ode-iha) to be made for the person to live long and prosper on earth.

What He Did to Become an Ifá Priest:

Moni moni osonju mona, odifa fun Òrúnmìlà baba n shawo
lo si Ifá. Akelu bebe tu be.

To know people is better than to know the way. That was the name of the Awo who made divination for Okonron-da-ase when he was going to practice as an Ifá priest at Ife. He was advised to make sacrifice with eight pigeons. He did the sacrifice and when he got to Ife, in accordance with the injunctions of his destiny, he married a new wife there. He became even more prosperous after the trip.

He Made Divination for the Furniture Seller Destined to Become Rich Within Three Years:

Bi agbagba meji ba ri ra won, wan kpitan kpitan.
Bi Babaláwo meji ba ri ra won, wan ki ran ki ran ran.
Bi ogbigbo meji ba ri ra won, wan ke ma huangan ma huangan.
Adifa fun Asigita ilu oyibo to maa la la la ti ti ti Odun meta.

When two elders meet, they narrate their experiences.

When two diviners meet, they will discuss Ifá interpretations and manifestations.
When two Toucans (bird) meet, they say to each other, Mahuangun Mahuangun.

These were the names of the Awos who made divination for the white furniture seller of Europe who was destined to become wealthy within a period of three years. He was told to make sacrifice with four pigeons, two Guinea fowls, one cock and one hen. He made the sacrifice and his furniture business became very lucrative.

At divination, the person should be told to make sacrifice in order to become wealthy through doing any business involving furniture, wood, or planks.

He Became a Member of the Ogboni Cult:

He was a crowed puller or group gatherer. On one occasion when his mother was not well, he sent for all the physicians in the area to help her, but they could not. He subsequently remembered the Ogboni fraternity and sent for them. They were called Awo Oshogbo. They came and succeeded in treating his mother to become well. They however told him that as soon as his mother was fully well, they should both arrange to be initiated into their cult.

After his mother got well, they both joined the cult. That is why as a mark of warning and identification, the Ogbonis use the expression - Ose-ounkan - which is an introverted way of pronouncing Okonron-Ose. It is a warning that the speaker has said enough and should stop instantly.

On one occasion however, Ifá advised him to stop attending the meeting because it was infested by witches, but that before stopping, he should make sacrifice with; a mother-sheep to Ifá, and two Guinea-fowls and two pigeons to his head. After the sacrifice, if they came to ask him why he stopped attending meetings, he was to explain that it was because he had changed his name from Okonron-ose to Okonron-wese and that he had washed the stigma of poverty from his head. He made the sacrifice.

When the day came for the next meeting, the agba drum began to beat the call sign of makpa! makpa! On three consecutive occasions, he did not respond to the invitation. The Ogbonis subsequently sent for him, but when they called him Okonron-Ose at the gate, he replied that he had changed his name to Okonron-wese and that he was no longer going to attend their meeting. With that, they left him alone.

At Ugbodu, the person should be warned to be wary about meetings. He should serve the new Ifa with two Guinea-fowls and a ram, and offer a cock to Ògún. At divination, the person should serve Ògún because of a meeting, and offer gifts to the Night.

Chapter Fifteen
Okonron-Ofun

```
I I    I I
 I     I I
I I    I I
 I      I
```

He Made Divination for Wealth (Ajé):

Okonron fifun kpeneden, Babaláwo aje, adifa fun aje.

He made divination for wealth when he was striving to have followership in the world. He also made divination for Onigede when he was striving to have money. They were both told to make sacrifice and they did. They made the sacrifice with white pigeons crushed yams and white cloth.

Meanwhile the Divinity of wealth left heaven in search of a suitable abode on earth. Onigede, the Oba of Igede had been advised to pluck the feathers of the white pigeon with which he made sacrifice and to add crushed yam (Elo or Ewo in Yorùbá and Obobo in Bini), and throw them round his palace, because those were the favorite food of wealth. When the representative daughter of Ajé stood at the boundry of heaven and earth to determine where to go, Èsù directed her to the house of Onigede where she saw all her staple requirements.

She moved into Onigede's house and settled down with all the wealth she brought from heaven. That was how Onigede became wealthy. At the height of his prosperity he made a feast for his subjects at which he sang and danced in praise of Òrúnmìlà.

When this Odù appears at divination for a man, he will be told that a woman, whether or not attractive, is coming to meet him. She is a harbinger or wealth. He should marry her because she has the key to the treasury of his prosperity.

If it appears for a woman, she will be told that she will travel to a place to marry a man who will make her happy.

He Made Divination for White Rabbits, Hares and Pigs:

Okonron fun fun fun, Awo emo, odifa fun emo, abufun Ehoro atun bu fun Esi, ati Elede.

He made divination for white rabbits, hare, bush pigs and domestic pigs. They were all told to make sacrifice each with a hen in order to have children on earth.

They all made sacrifice and began to have plenty of children. That is why they mutter sounds in praise of Okonron fun-fun-fun to this day. At divination, the person should make sacrifice to have children.

He Made Divination for Òrìsà-Nlá, Oshereigbo:

Okonron fifun kpeneden, odifa fun Òrìsà-Nlá Oshereigbo.

He made divination for God's representative on earth, when he was coming to the world. He was told to make sacrifice in order to command the honor and respect of all divinities and mankind. He made sacrifice with two white pigeons, a white hen and white cloth. That was why on earth, he commanded universal honor and respect. Whenever he appeared, all would shout "Ba ta laoo."

At divination, the person will be told to make sacrifice in order to become honorable and respectable.

Sacrifice for Prosperity:

Ewe di ewe, di'le di'le mi, di ona iku fun mi, maa di ona ire.

Leaves upon leaves offer protection. Close the way to death for me, but do not close the path to prosperity. When this Odù appears at divination, the person should be told to make sacrifice with a pig and a pigeon for eternal prosperity.

He Made Divination for the Monkey:

Okonron mofun, Okonron mofun, Okonron fi sere sere, Babaláwo
edun, odifa fun edun nigbati o nbe ninu ikamo awon omo eran ko ko.

He made divination for the Monkey when the more ferocious animals vowed that the monkey would never have any ground to stand upon and that they would always hunt and kill her and her children. That was when she ran to Òrúnmìlà who advised her to make sacrifice with food, egusi soup, scarf, and a big he-goat. After making the sacrifice for the Monkey, Òrúnmìlà told her to use the prepared food to feast the big trees of the forest. She did as she was told.

After feasting the trees, they asked her for the purpose of making the sacrifice and Èsù replied on her behalf. Èsù told them that the stronger animals had declared an eternal war against Alakedun, resolving to kill her and her children from generation to generation. That is why Òrúnmìlà advised her to seek affinity with the trees to grant her refuge and solace whenever she was threatened. After explaining the purpose of the feast, Èsù enjoined all the trees to bend down their branches to lift up the monkey any time she and her children required succor. The trees not only promised to oblige, but unanimously proclaimed that even if it is their leaves the monkey hangs on to, the leaves would never cut. They should be able to give the necessary support to the monkey.

That is why to this day, the traditional habitat of the monkey is on top of trees, because of the concordat their ancestral mother entered into, with the trees at the beginning of time. The only tree that did not participate in the monkey's feast was a tree called Iyere in Yorùbá, which is why no monkey goes near it for any reason whatsoever.

When this Odù appears at divination, the person will be advised to make sacrifice, and to make a feast for his neighbors, so that himself and his family do not become victims of unforeseen contingencies.

The Divination He Made Before Leaving Heaven:

Fifun la ti ri asho fifun.
Pipon la ti ri asho pupa.
Didun la ti ri asho didun.

Those were the three Awos who made divination for Okonron-mo-Ofun when he was leaving heaven.

He was advised to make sacrifice to avoid having problems with women on earth, more especially, not to die on account on a woman. He was told to serve his guardian angel with a black goat, black cloth, fish, rat, two bags of money, and a gourd of respectable wine (in modern parlance, a bottle of alcoholic spirit). He was to serve his head with white cock, white cloth, white eagle's feather, and coconut. He was also to serve Ògún with red cock, red cloth and a gourd of palm wine. Finally, he was to serve Èsù with he-goat, white, red, and black cloth and crushed yam.

He was too poor to afford the cost of such elaborate sacrifices. His guardian angel however advised him to borrow money to fund the cost of the sacrifices and to repay the loan when he became prosperous on earth. He followed the advice of his guardian angel and left for the world after making the sacrifices.

On getting to the world, he took to trading and hunting, and completely ignored Ifá practice. He had the regular routine of beginning his day by wearing white clothes to pray to God. In the afternoon, he would put on red clothes to pray to Ògún to help him achieve his mission on earth. In the evening he often wore black clothes and prayed to his guardian angel not to allow his enemies to kill him under cover of darkness.

One day, a gang of robbers burglarized the king's palace and removed all the regal jewelry and hid them by the side of a tree in the heart of the forest. When Okonron-mo-Ofun went hunting in the forest, he found the jewelry-dump, and without touching them, he returned home to ask Ifá what to do about the find. He was advised to give a he-goat quickly to Èsù so that the jewels might still be there by the time he returned to the forest.

Incidentally, he mentioned it to his wife, who immediately hatched her own plans for collecting the jewels for herself. She went to her boyfriend, to arrange to lay an ambush against her and to seize her from the husband, so they could both kill him after seizing the jewels from him. As she was going to the forest with her husband, they were attacked by three men, who immediately seized her, while attacking him and falling him to the ground. After falling him to the ground, they left for the jewelry-dump, but since they did not know the place, Èsù blocked their approach and diverted their attention elsewhere.

Meanwhile, Okonron-mo-Ofun got up and went alone to collect the jewels to his house. Much later in the day, the three men and Okonron-mo-Ofun's wife got to the tree described to her by the husband. It was the right place, but they came too late, because Okonron-mo-Ofun had beaten them to it. While they were fidgeting around in search of the jewels, the robbers who kept them by the side of the tree came round and accused them of stealing their goods. A fight ensured in which they used poisoned arrows against one another. All the combatants died on the spot, including Okonron-mo- Ofun's wife. Okonron-mo-Ofun became very prosperous, and later, he was able to repay the loan he took to make sacrifice in heaven.

When this Ifá appears at Ugbodu, the above-mentioned sacrifices should be made without delay to avoid being killed by a woman. He is destined to be enriched by someone else's wealth. The special sacrifice is made with a black goat, white, red and black cloth and the heads of parrot and eagle.

He Made Divination for the Corpse:

advised the corpse to make sacrifice with dried materials and to give he-goat to Èsù, so that at death he would neither smell nor rot. He refused to make the sacrifice.

Meanwhile, the Divinity of Death was queried by Èsù why he was allowing the corpse to continue to move about with the living, after death. Èsù proclaimed that the corpse should from then on, get rotten and decay. At the same time, death invited all the heavenly police for a feast, and the corpse was among those invited. The corpse ate and drank and became drunk. When he swooned into delirium tremens, he fell to the ground and the people began to pour water on his body, when in fact he forbade water either for drinking or for bathing.

When he regained consciousness, he discovered that water had been poured on him. His body began to change texture and within three days, began to go rotten and to smell, which made people to start distancing themselves away from him. That is why no one likes to go near the corpse to this day and why it decays.

He Made Divination for Oro, the Divinity of Secrecy:

He made divination for Oro not to throw the missile with which he declares a curfew in order to avoid the danger of getting lost. He did not heed the advice. He went ahead to throw his missile which resulted in his getting lost in the forest. Consequently, his annual festival suddenly ground to a halt.

The following year, Oro was not available to perform his annual festival. When his followers could not find him, they went to Okonron-mo-Ofun who advised them to make sacrifice with kolanut and palm wine.

After the sacrifice, his followers went in search of him. They eventually met him at the foot of a tree in the forest and told him that his friend Okonron-mo-Ofun and all his admirers wanted him to return home. He agreed to return home with them. As he was getting close to the town, he shouted Okonron-mo-Ofun, mofun mofun.

When he remembered that he was naked, he ran back to the forest. He gave them the knife with which he declares the curfew and told his followers to be using it to invoke him from heaven, to which he returned.

At Ugbodu, the person should be advised to serve his home town's divinity, having Oro, with a dog. At divination, the person should give cock to Ògún, and he-goat to Èsù, to avoid getting lost out of foolhardiness.

Other titles by C. Osamaro Ibie

Ibie, C. Osamaro
IFISM: THE COMPLETE WORKS OF ORUNMILA
251pp. 2 b/w, 11 line, Illust. Cloth

Ibie, C. Osamaro
IFISM: THE COMPLETE WORKS OF ORUNMILA
VOL. 2-THE ODUS OF EJI-OGBE
HOW MAN CREATED HIS OWN GOD
242pp. 5 b/w, 41 line, Illust.

Ibie, C. Osamaro
IFISM: THE COMPLETE WORKS OF ORUNMILA
VOL. 3-THE ODUS OF OYEKU-MEJI
101pp. 1 b/w

Ibie, C. Osamaro
IFISM: THE COMPLETE WORKS OF ORUNMILA
VOL. 4-THE ODUS OF IWORI
172pp. 1 b/w

Ibie, C. Osamaro
IFISM: THE COMPLETE WORKS OF ORUNMILA
VOL. 5-THE ODUS OF IDI
144pp. 1 b/w

www.ingramcontent.com/pod-product-compliance
Lightning Source LLC
Chambersburg PA
CBHW080744300426
44114CB00019B/2646